Prejudice and the People of God:

Racial Reconciliation Rooted in Redemption and Guided by Revelation

Dear Beverly,

I appreciate meeting you.

May God bless you!

Dr. A. Charles Ware

Dr. A Charles Ware

Jn 13: 34-35

Edited by Eugene Seals

A Quality Book™

Prejudice and the People of God:
Racial Reconciliation Rooted in Redemption and
Guided by Revelation

Published by

Baptist Bible College of Indianapolis
601 N. Shortridge Road
Indianapolis, IN 46219
317-352-8736

Copyright © 1998 by Dr. A. Charles Ware

Unless otherwise indicated, Scripture quotations are from the King James Version.

Editing and typography by
Eugene Seals
Quality Publishing Systems
Box 339635
Farmington Hills, MI 48333

Printed in the United States of America

Contents

Dedication

To my godly wife, Sharon, who for 25 years has been a Christian sister, friend, excellent wife and mother, and has shown me love through my times of struggle and growth in the area of racial reconciliation.

Chapter 1 – Racial Reconciliation: Past Present, and Future

It is refreshing to see the growing interest in racial reconciliation within the Church. God is stirring the hearts of many to seek to demonstrate the love and unity which the Bible says should characterize the children of God. Although interest has greatly increased in building better relationships between different races, there is still a great need for clarity on many of the issues relating to biblical reconciliation. Biblical unity in the midst of diversity is not as easy as some would like to think.

The thought of blended cultures in the Church provokes a multiplicity of questions: Is this another humanistic liberal attempt to unify the world? Is this a mere mimicking of civil rights issues? Is this entire discussion a defection to the so-called social gospel? Don't people of different races prefer to be with their own? With all the problems people with similar backgrounds and cultures are having, why add a new set of problems? Can people from different backgrounds really worship together? How do you attract minorities to predominantly white member organizations and keep them? What about interracial marriage?

The multiplicity of questions provides strong incentives for giving attention to the issue of racial reconciliation. For too long the Church has treated the whole issue of race relations as an unmentionable subject! As a result, many saints are genuinely confused regarding what God has to say on the issue. This lack of a clear word from God leaves many believers perplexed concerning what practical steps they can take to live in obedience to God in respect to those different from themselves.

Many Christians – as well as some non-Christians – have rightly discerned that much of the talk about multiculturalism, pluralism, diversity, race relations, and the like is creating more division than unity. Furthermore, there is a lack of an objective moral standard by which to judge the issues. Diversity has been divested of any moral foundation. Love has been redefined as abhorring that which is good while cleaving to that which is evil.

The God Who Comforts Us

As Christians, our message must move beyond merely pointing to the errors of the world; we must proclaim and practice the truth of Scripture! The Christian, unlike the world, has a clear guide for racial reconciliation.

The implementation of these biblical principles within a multiethnic or multicultural environment will require commitment. We must learn to listen, to forgive, to educate, and to encourage one another. We must each work hard to correct the errors of the past. Whatever one's race, believers need to pray together, persevere, share, and provoke one another to love and good works.

We desperately need to recognize that the Church is God's possession, purchased with the blood of Christ. Christians, therefore, need to search the Scripture together to find God's solution to the "race issue."

Confronting the Sin of Racism

There needs to be a standard by which one can discern these issues. Since the Church is the possession of God and believers are only stewards, it is God's prerogative to define what our relationships should be (Acts 20:28; Ephesians 1:21-23). The mind of God is revealed in Scripture (2 Timothy 3:14-16). True Christians should have three primary concerns. The first should be to determine what the Scripture teaches (2 Timothy 2:15). This should be discerned through a literal, grammatical, and historical interpretation of biblical texts addressing the issue. Second, after the primary interpretation of Scripture, application needs to be made to the present historical cultural setting in which one is living. Third, all Scripture properly understood and applied demands a response from the believer (James 1:21-25).

One of the great challenges to finding an acceptable prescription for racism is the lack of a clear definition of the disease. We may begin with Webster's definition of racism:

The assumption that the characteristics and abilities of an individual are determined by race and that one race is biologically superior to another. A political program or social system based on this assumption.

The Scripture has spoken to this assumption. Respect of persons is sin (Deuteronomy 1:16-17; 16:19; Acts 10:26-28, 34-35; Galatians 2:6; Colossians 3:25). Sin in the Church is a major, not a minor, issue. Churches have fled from neighborhoods because of ethnic change. In their flight, the Gospel has been withdrawn also. This action is in direct disobedience to the command to "Go into all the world and make disciples of all nations...." The evangelization of the lost is a major biblical issue which has been, in some cases, color-coded. Certain colors have been deemed worthy of the Gospel while others have been deemed unworthy. Certainly this is respect of persons.

The Church was not only commanded to make disciples, but also to baptize believers in the name of the Father, Son, and Holy Spirit. There has been more than one pastor who has shared with me instances where Bible-believing churches refused to even allow a black person to be baptized in "their" baptistry.

The final biblical command in the Great Commission is that the new disciples were to be taught all things whatsoever Christ had commanded. Yet there have been denial of admission to churches, mission agencies, Christian schools, Bible colleges, and seminaries based upon one's color or ethnic background. And still these institutions hope to become instruments of healing. Certainly such actions should be considered respect of persons. The growing number of public confessions and resolutions concerning past acts of commission and omission at least brings to public attention that these things were done. At the same time, it should be noted that many of those making the confessions are acknowledging acts of the past with which they never agreed and were never involved.

Defining racism as respect of persons and sin still fails to give the Church clear direction for bringing about healing and reconciliation. This is due in part to the use of generalizations and stereotypes which seek only to cast blame or prove innocence. The Church's vocation should be, rather, to approach the subject in humility, endeavoring to keep the unity of the Spirit in the bond of peace. Some blacks consider all whites to be racists. This lacks historical integrity. There were whites involved in the abolition movement, the underground railroad, the civil rights struggle, and so forth. Without the aid of such individuals, those movements would not have achieved the results that they did. Even today there are large numbers of white Christians and non-Christians who are promoting racial reconciliation.

On the other hand, some whites believe that blacks were only leaches, making no real contribution to Christianity in America. However, again, such generalization lacks historical integrity. There were black preachers of the Gospel in the 1700s. Black missionaries such as Lott Carey left American soil as early as 1821, predating such white missionary legends as William Carey and Adoniram Judson. Carey wrote:

> *I am an African, and in this country (USA), however meritorious my conduct and respectable my character, I cannot receive the credit due to either. I wish to go to a country where I shall be estimated by my merits, not by my complexion; and I feel bound to labor for my suffering race.* (Fitts, pages 19-20)

Discernment is easier when broad generalizations and stereotypes are not used as the grid through which personal application is sifted. Pride may naturally pervert our judgment. Sometimes nothing unites as quickly as a common enemy. Therefore, some Christians have found it comfortable to talk about "them and us" or blacks and whites as irreconcilable enemies rather than as family members seeking biblical solutions to family problems.

The mature believer realizes that both the acquiring and the application of biblical wisdom take effort. As a Bible college professor shared his life verse: Proverbs 11:1 says that "A false balance is an abomination to the Lord, but a just weight is his delight." Balance is beautiful but very difficult to find and maintain in this world of sin. There is perhaps no greater area where wisdom and balance is needed in the Church than in the area of biblical relationships between believers of differing ethnic or cultural backgrounds.

It has been said that either sin will keep you from the Word or the Word will keep you from sin. It is a biblical fact that the Word of God can and should cleanse saints from sin (Psalm 119:9; John 17:17; 1 Peter 2:1-2; Hebrews 4:12). But how is this to be reconciled with the fact that a number of biblical scholars and leaders have preached and practiced "racism." Perhaps racism is biblical. Or, maybe, it is just a secular, humanistic concept with little or no relevance to the Church. Some Christians have taken the principle promoted by scientific creationist Ken Ham that race is an evolutionary rather than a biblical concept. A few of these Christians thus argue that any discussion of racism is, therefore, unbiblical. (Ken Ham, however, does not follow his principle to this conclusion.) Other Christians see race relations as a minor issue that the Church must not become involved with to the neglect of the major issues.

Many discussions of the race problem in America generate more heat than light. What is needed is to hear from God and to be responsive to His position on the matter.

Chapter 2 – Social, Secular, and Religious Tenets of Reconciliation

There is no end to the number of critical challenges facing our society. Racial reconciliation is one of them. President Clinton is seeking to engage the nation in further discussion on the race issue. He has formed a seven-member advisory board for that purpose. Many Christians, as well as some non-Christians, have rightly discerned that much of the talk about multiculturalism, pluralism, diversity, and the like may be creating more division than unity. S. D. Gaede puts it eloquently:

> *With few exceptions, multiculturalism is not argued today on the basis of promoting justice but on the grounds of inclusiveness. And the fundamental assumption is that it is good to be tolerant of different ideas and different perspectives. In other words, undergirding current thought on multiculturalism is not some sense of what is ultimately just and true, but a very deep moral and ontological relativism. Thus the argument for multiculturalism typically runs like this: Because all cultural perspectives are equally valid, every idea or perspective ought to be included. Indeed, to be exclusive about truth (to assert that one can distinguish between truth and error) is bad, while to be inclusive of all truth claims is good.* (page 37)

As noted in chapter 1, in the name of tolerance, we as a society are becoming increasingly more intolerant of Bible-believing Christians. Diversity has been divested of any objective moral foundation. Love has been redefined as abhorring that which is good while cleaving to that which is evil. When man unites in rebellion against God, the consequences will be severe. (See Genesis 10 and 2 Thessalonians 2:1-12.)

But as Christians, our message must move beyond merely pointing to the errors of the world. We must manifest the message of the Word! What should the Christian response to racial reconciliation be? Certainly not this year's model. Gaede laments the current state of affairs:

> *In the midst of this confusion, however, stands a united church, offering the culture an alternative vision: a vision rooted not in the turmoil of the times but the values of the kingdom.... I'm afraid not. Too often what we find among Christians today is the same confusion, containing some biblical insights, perhaps, but mostly parroting the arguments of the day.* (page 15)

The Christian, unlike the world, has a clear guide for racial reconciliation, and that is Divine revelation – the Bible. What is the message of the Bible in regard to reconciliation? God in His sovereign wisdom has established a unity between believers – regardless of racial or cultural background – which is expressed in several ways in Ephesians 2:11-22.

If God has created such a marvelous relationship for believers, why are there not more models within the Christian community? What is our responsibility? The Scripture charges us with the responsibility to endeavor to keep the unity (Ephesians 4:3). Biblical reconciliation is threatened and thwarted by personal and corporate sin as well as by doctrinal defection. To properly nurture and grow in the unity which God has created, true believers must be committed to the clear teaching of Scripture, to biblical morality, and to divine love. Racial recon-

ciliation in the Church is a high calling. Let us seek to walk
worthy of such a calling. The challenge is to show the compassion of Christ without compromising the truth of Christ.
True racial reconciliation is rooted in redemption and
guided by revelation, God's Holy Bible. At Baptist Bible College of Indianapolis (BBCI), we model the message of reconciliation with an integrated board, staff, and student body. The
question for Christians is simply, "What does the Scripture
say?" To seek the answer to that question, Ken Davis, a white
professor, and I explore the theoretical underpinnings of racial
reconciliation through a course entitled "Race, Culture, and the
Church." That class is in large part the inspiration for this
book. I am thankful to God for the privilege of partnering with
a cross-cultural staff at an institution committed to racial reconciliation. I appreciate the input and stimulation at BBCI and
the vision of Christians like Ken Davis and Dr. Clinton Kaul-
feld, who with the late Dr. James S. Wells founded BBCI in
1980.

The Voice of Biblical Reconciliation

One evening I was watching one of the news shows which
featured a debate between a fundamental white Christian leader
and a black leader. As the two leaders argued various view-
points concerning racial issues, I listened intently. Integration
of schools became the focal point of the discussion. At one
point in the debate, the fundamental Christian commented
something to the effect, "If they want to go to college, they
have their own university down the street!" I wondered, "am I
one of *them* because I'm black, who had my university down
the street, or was his Christian university for me, too, a Christian who happens to be black?" I was left with the impression
that I belonged with blacks without reference to my faith.

The comment both shocked and enraged me. I wondered,
how many blacks in the Washington, D.C., area and around the

country heard that statement. How could I proclaim a message of reconciliation to God and to our brothers in Christ when my brother just excluded me from the number of the redeemed? It was that night that I determined something must be done. The scriptural message must gain a greater hearing, if blacks were not to be alienated from the Gospel. Shortly after watching that program I gathered some local pastors together and we formed The Voice of Biblical Reconciliation. The following is a statement which we drafted to express our commitment to lift our voices against racism in the Church.

Many of us have heard accounts of unbiblical practices among Bible-believing Christians when it comes to the race issue. Many of us have spent many hours discussing the biblical inequities and the serious consequences these practices have produced both within and outside the church. Some of us have even preached or taught on the subject at times. But all too often we have been silent. Silent while we have watched others suffer. Silent, while we ourselves have suffered! The suffering would not seem so bad if it were from the hand of the world. But it came from the hand of our brethren who profess to believe the Word. Our silence would be more understandable if it were practiced by those seeking to silence the Word – but the silence is by many of us who profess a conviction that the entire Word of God must be proclaimed.

In 1982, a group of burdened Bible-believing pastors decided that the silence must be broken for the clarity of our own consciences. For the cause of Christ among blacks, other minorities, and the total body of Christ, we felt that we must take action on this grave issue at this critical hour of history. The Voice of Biblical Reconciliation was organized to give hope to many blacks and other minority brethren who feel betrayed and isolated. We want to educate many of our brethren – black, white, and others

– to the seriousness of this issue. We desire to create a vehicle for reconciliation for all Christians who share like precious faith, but who remain segregated merely because of race – that Christ might be exalted and that the Word of God might have free course.

The Voice of Biblical Reconciliation is open to people of all races. We seek to have a healing effect upon the Body of Christ. We share the desire of the Apostle Paul as expressed in Philippians 2:1-4:

"If there be, therefore, any consolation in Christ, if any comfort of love, if any fellowship of the Spirit, if any tender mercies and compassions, fulfill ye my joy, that ye be likeminded, having the same love, being of one accord, of one mind. Let nothing be done through strife or vainglory, but in lowliness of mind let each esteem others better than themselves. Look not every man on his own things, but every man also on the things of others."

We acknowledge that advances have been made. But truth is still being shackled by traditional prejudice. We pray that the coming generation will not have to endure the pain which many in this generation have had to face simply because there was not an effective Voice of Biblical Reconciliation.

Need for Action

Several of us who believed that the time for action had come created the Voice of Biblical Reconciliation to give voice to our concerns. Since that time many more voices addressing the race issue are being heard. Yet, the battle has just begun. The people of God must purge themselves from prejudice. We must cross the color line for the sake of the evangelization of the lost and edification of the saints. The testimony of the Church, with respect to race relations, before a watching world must be improved.

For too long the Church has avoided the issue of race relations. As a result, many saints are genuinely confused as to what God has to say on the issue and what practical steps one can take to live in obedience to God. Groups like the Ku Klux Klan and the Black Muslims draw converts by appealing to racial superiority and injustice arguments. The Church must be prepared to give an answer for the hope that lies within us.

It is refreshing to see the nation begin to discuss the race issue again. However, it is the Church that should take the lead and show the way. We must continue to explore and explain racial reconciliation from both practical and biblical perspectives.

The Church is being given another chance to correct its errors of the past and to chart a new path for the future. Isn't God good! It is time to stand and speak forth the Word of God. It is time for the Church to adorn herself with love – a love that pursues and sacrifices for relationships which reflect the wisdom of God in constituting a multiethnic Church.

Every saint has a responsibility. Christian pastors and teachers must explain the Scripture's affirmation of unity in Christ. Christian families must train their children to love and respect all people. Christian businesses must financially support efforts toward reconciliation. Christian organizations and businesses must work hard to weed out prejudice in principle and/or practice. Individuals and organizations must work at creating cross-cultural partnerships.

I firmly believe that God has prepared His Church for such a time as this. A failure to act now would be a lost opportunity. An attempt to delegate this issue to the next generation would be irresponsible. The time for action is now.

As we examine the issues related to biblical reconciliation, there are several biblical principles which we desire to follow:

1. The Bible speaks to every critical issue of our Christian life and relationships (2 Timothy 3:16-17).
2. Biblical truths and Holy Spirit-energized works are to have pre-eminence over one's culture or heritage (John 4:23-24).
3. All of mankind are sinners in need of a Savior (Romans 3:9-23).
4. Jesus Christ is the only Savior for all mankind (Romans 3:24-30).
5. True salvation makes one a part of the family of God, which is composed of true believers from every people group (John 3:16; 1 Corinthians 12:13-14; Ephesians 2:13-22; Revelation 7:9).
6. If we dig deeply enough, all of our roots will eventually lead us to Noah and Adam (Genesis 1:26-27; 8, 9; Acts 17:26-29).
7. The Bible exhorts us to unity with diversity (Ephesians 4:1-6).
8. The early Church had to address this issue (Acts 6:1-7; 10; 11; 15; Galatians 2:1-16).
9. Love for the brethren is a mark of true believers (1 John 3:14-18; 4:7-11).
10. Christians' love for one another should cause the world to know that we are disciples of Christ (John 13:34-35).
11. We all need biblical humility as we communicate to each other (Philippians 2:1-8).
12. We need to listen to each other.
13. We need to forgive each other.
14. We need to correct the errors of the past.
15. We need to pray.
16. We need to persevere.
17. We need to share.
18. We need to provoke one another to love and good works.
19. We need to recognize that the Church is God's possession, purchased with the blood of Christ.

We should follow His counsel regarding the makeup of the Church.

Simple vs. Complex

Jesus is the answer to the race problem. Christians boldly proclaim that Jesus is the answer to all of society's problems. Billboards read JESUS IS THE ANSWER. Popular Christian songs fill the airways with the simplicity of the answer as well. Consider the message of this contemporary song:

> Jesus is the answer
> to the world today.
> For me there is no other.
> Jesus is the way.   André Crouch

The cure for racism, as for all sin, is both simple and complex. The simplicity is found in the reality that Christ, by his death, burial and resurrection, has paid the full price for sin. No matter how terrible one's sin may have been, upon trusting Christ as Lord and Savior, full forgiveness is granted (Ephesians 1:7; 2:1-9). Beyond forgiveness, the righteousness of Christ (His life of sinless perfection) is charged to the repentant sinner's account (Romans 3:21-26; 2 Corinthians 5:21). Through faith alone, a sinner is forgiven all of his sins and credited with the sinless life of Christ. This is a simple, yet profound, transaction! Theologians call it *positional sanctification*. It is called positional because it speaks of what we possess by virtue of the fact that we are in Christ (Romans 8:29-30; 1 Corinthians 1:30; Ephesians 1:3-4).

Yet, racism, as well as other sins, has been present among Christians. If Jesus is the answer, why does racism still exist within the family of God? How could the Church watch silently while the cruelties of slavery and racial injustice were legally perpetrated upon citizens of this great country? Did Jesus direct the Church to form segregated assemblies and hostile relationships? Why is it that confessions of past racism, new resolutions, and national conferences on racial reconciliation have not solved the problem?

The complexity of the issue has to do with human personality, which has been corrupted by sin. At the time of salvation, we are forgiven of our sin; but we have not been instantly freed from all of its power. Personal freedom from sin is a *process.* Theologians call this process of removing sin from one's life "progressive sanctification." The speed with which one replaces sinful behavior with righteous behavior is dependent upon a number of factors.

Pride is one challenge in reversing racism into radical love. Natural to the human heart is the aspiration to be better than others. This attitude lends itself to grouping by color wherein people compete to show themselves superior through education, wealth, or morality. Pride makes it difficult to confess or forgive sins of the past. Pride is more interested in casting blame than constructing solutions. Prejudice prospers in the midst of a proud people.

One of the many faces of pride is fear. Fear of confrontation, contention, and possible failure turn the weak of heart away from the path of victory. The fear of doctrinal defection and race pollution through interracial marriage paralyzes many saints. Others fear retaliation, loss of control, neglect of disadvantaged peoples, and closed doors to ministry opportunities. To say that there are insecurity and a lack of trust between the saints would be an understatement. Fear weakens faith; and small faith fails to see the greatness of God in the midst of giants, such as a racially divided Church.

A second challenge is approximately two hundred years of lies and injustices coming from high places in the land. Two good books on this subject are *Lies My Teacher Told Me* and *Our Racist Legacy: Will the Church Resolve the Conflict?* We are still living with the residue of a culture of blatant deceit. The consequence is distrust. One wonders whether discussion of race relations is an honest desire for a cure or merely an attempt to cover up present inequities. Racism has flowed through the American culture like blood through the human body. Healing racism will be neither fast nor painless.

Third is the fact that reconciliation comes at a high price. Reconcilers are sometimes misunderstood and alienated by each group they are seeking to reconcile. The reconcilers are called names and falsely accused. Their loyalty to Christ is questioned, and saints are told to separate from them. Doors of opportunity are closed. They become saints without a family. Often, lonely is the road toward reconciliation. Few there be that will trust Christ and press forward, cutting a new path through the confusion of secular multiculturalism and sacred pride.

Fourth is the problem of sorting through the moral relativism of the culture, confronting the unrighteous while affirming righteousness. The Church, by and large, has been *reacting* to issues in society. As a result, more of our energy is spent exposing the error of secular pluralism than proclaiming racial reconciliation. Secular pluralism has joined race, gender, and sexual orientation together in unholy matrimony. The heat of this national debate makes it difficult for Christians to clarify how they may affirm racial and gender equity while seeing sexual orientation as a moral issue. The scarcity of racial and gender reconciliation models weakens the impact of our message.

Racial reconciliation becomes a challenge when two groups have developed along diverse and often competitive historical paths. Sadly, historical literature which is to be taught to coming generations is tainted by the racist bias, or ignorance, of those who control the curricula. Questions concerning who the role models are and what values should be emphasized in history become a challenge in a racially divided land. Truth and integrity demand great discernment in our multicultural environment.

It has proven beneficial for me to determine to which of several groups an individual belongs and then to communicate on the basis of that knowledge.

Racists are people who, like the Nazis, refuse to listen to any evidence which contradicts their bias. These people are usually open and vocal about their innate racial superiority. They need an unusual work of grace.

Prejudiced people have made a judgment without all the data. When given more data, a prejudiced person may change.

Perplexed individuals are confused by the entire racial discussion. They tend to be very sensitive and are constantly concerned about saying or doing something to offend someone. They need to be loved and handled gently.

The *protective* person is usually a parent whose greatest concern is that they do not want their children to get involved in the racial debate for fear they may be hurt. Protective persons fail to understand that Christianity often calls for suffering. To suffer for righteousness is a privilege granted to some of us by our heavenly Father.

The *positioned* person, like the Apostle Peter, supports segregation due to his or her belief that the Scripture teaches it. This person, like Peter, needs to hear a clear defense of racial reconciliation from the Bible. He may well require more than one hearing.

Fifth is the lack of common definitions and expectations. blacks and whites differ greatly on what constitutes racism, the seriousness of the issue, and the solutions. Is racism an attitude, a belief, an action, a look, a structure, an environment, a method, or a combination of all of these? How can we solve a problem which we cannot define? There is a great need for objective goals that both groups believe to be attainable and just.

Finally, what makes racial reconciliation a complex matter for the Church is the fact that the Bible has been misinterpreted and misapplied. This miseducation of the people of God led many to believe that racism and many of its accompanying cruelties were sanctioned by God. Today we see that, although many leaders of Christian organizations have rejected the racist teaching of past leaders, their institutions were established upon racist premises. To some, it is sacrilegious to expose the errors of deceased founders and work to conform the institution to a biblical standard. This may affect curricula, history, and policies. It is much easier to deny integrity and defend the past, even if it is not exactly the truth.

Regardless of the complexity of the issue, we need a generation of leaders with integrity – leaders with clear consciences who honor God above all others – leaders who exalt truth above tradition – leaders who will study, teach and live the Scripture faithfully – leaders who will persevere through opposition and disappointment.

Reconciliation leaders realize that the source of the solution is simple, but the outworking is complex. The Bible is clear that the Church should be like a spectacular rainbow in the midst of a dark and dreary society. But harmonious relationships between people of differing ethnic origins is proving to be difficult to attain. Dreams of loving multiethnic ministries have been replaced by nightmares of competitive, contentious, confrontational meeting that have ended in deeper divisions.

Racial reconciliation will not be easy, but it is achievable. Believers must make the commitment to learn from both the past and the present in order to build a better future. We must be more open about critical issues that divide us, with the goal of finding solutions rather than casting blame. We must be willing to fail in our pursuit of victory without quitting until our unity causes our community to believe that we are disciples of Christ because of our manifest love for one another.

The time has come for action. May this indeed be the generation of biblical racial reconciliation.

Why should this generation succeed when others have failed? Success will come from the fact that God is raising up a generation who believe reconciliation to be a biblical or theological rather than a social or cultural issue as it has been considered. One pastor has rightly observed that, "The Word of God supersedes politics, supersedes people, supersedes race."

Commitment to a Literal Grammatical Historical Interpretation

The Bible is the authoritative, exclusive Word of God. 2 Timothy 3:16 puts it this way, "All Scripture is given by inspiration of God and is profitable for doctrine, reproof, correction, and instruction in righteousness." The phrase, "inspiration of God," is one word in Greek, the original language of the New Testament. The word literally means *God breathed.* The idea is that the Scripture comes from the very mouth of God. Other Scriptures support this concept, too.

Therefore, the task of any interpreter of Scripture is not to correct the text. This would be, in fact to correct God. Rather, one should approach the text to discover from it the mind of God. The mind of God is discovered by diligently searching for the historical grammatical meaning of the text. Simply, stated the meaning of any biblical text must be determined by what the text communicated in the historical/cultural context in which it was written. Integrity with the text would require that sound rules of grammar be applied also to determine accurately what the author was saying.

Theologically, such an approach to the Scripture is called the grammatical historical method of interpretation. This approach allows the Bible, the Word of God, to stand in judgment of men rather than men standing in judgment over the Word of God. Thus the Bible is authoritative and accurate; but man's interpretation and application of Scripture must always be critiqued by a proper understanding of the text itself.

The Bible does not need to be cleansed of cultural or racial bias. Because of a misinterpretation and misapplication of certain biblical texts, the resulting confusion concerning what is the mind of God on race relations has led some to charge that the Bible itself is erroneous at points. The Nation of Islam charges that Christianity is the white man's religion. A friend from the Ojibwa Nation has a manuscript with that very title: "The White Man's Religion." His purpose is to counteract that notion among his people. The struggle with the reliability of the Scripture in relationship to racial issues can be seen among Christians as well as among those of different religious persuasions. Latta Thomas makes a passionate appeal for blacks to read the Bible:

... to reach the minds and hearts of Black people in America ... who would like to see in the biblical tradition at least a measure of what many of their fore parents discerned in it but who have some honest doubts and suspicions due to the ways the Bible has been misinterpreted and manipulated to support Black oppression. The greatest tragedy that could happen to Black people in a day when full liberation is the password is to have them pass up the greatest collective document of human liberation that has ever come out of human experience and the effort of God. Black people must find out for themselves ... what the Bible is really about. For it is a book in which it is recorded that the *God and Sovereign of all history is always in the business of creating and freeing a people to clear the earth of injustice, bigotry, hatred, human slavery, political corruption, tyranny, sin, illness, and poverty. It is a book in which*

there is an invitation to all people who will hear and respond to put all else aside and join God in the job of renewing the earth, believing that it must and can be done. (pages 12-13)

While Thomas' appeal is to be applauded, there is a word of caution concerning his method of handling some biblical texts. In his explanation of certain passages he denies or questions the historical reliability of the text.

Dr. Cain Hope Felder, chairman of the Department of New Testament Studies at Howard University, is to be commended for his dedication and scholarly work. I have personally benefited from his writing and tapes. However, one must be cautious when following scholars who question the authority and veracity of the Word of God. In his groundbreaking *Troubling Biblical Waters: Race, Class, and Family,* Felder asserted:

People must seek to liberate themselves from the popular tendency to deify the Bible as the definitive and exclusive Word of God, as if God's entire revelation only exists in the canon of biblical literature. (1989, page 14)

Dr. Jeremiah A. Wright, Jr., and Rev. Carmen Kates prepared a study guide for Felder's scholarly *Troubling Biblical Waters.* The purpose of the study guide is to help laymen understand the message of the book which is written for scholars. Felder uses the higher critical method of biblical interpretation as indicated on pages 4 and 5 of the study guide. There is no argument that the Bible has been misused and abused by many to legitimize inhumane and unjust treatment of human beings. Blacks have been stolen, separated from family, beaten, enslaved, raped, and murdered – all under the banner of obedience to the Word of God.

Writings of the slavery period indicate that such actions were based on a variety of motives – from a denial that black

men had souls to an attempt to keep the white gene pool pure
Nevertheless, these errors are not corrected by a denial that we
possess an accurate copy of the Word of God. Good reading in this
connection would be Craig S. Keener and Glenn Usry's *Black
Men's Religion: Can Christianity Be Afrocentric?* (InterVarsity,
1996).

The issue is not whether stories and teachings which are in
the Bible for all to read should be there or not. The text does
not need to be cleansed from cultural and/or racial bias. It is
man's misinterpretation and misapplication of the Bible that
needs to be cleansed from cultural and/or racial bias. Misinterpretation leads to misapplication, which leads to misdirection.
The examples previously cited clearly illustrate the misuse and
abuse of blacks based upon wrongly dividing the Word of
Truth. Such treatment and teachings fostered a lack of respect
of people not only by others but also among blacks themselves.
Thus a new generation is fighting for dignity and respect by
throwing off the restraints imposed upon them by white European and European American scholars. This new generation is
seeking truth free of the contamination of racist bias.

There is a growing enthusiasm today among black Christians about the discovery of blacks in the Bible. Arguments are
surfacing that the first man, Adam, was black. Some white
brethren have been offended by pictures depicting Jesus as
black. Further frustration and unbelief is manifested when one
flips through the *Original African Heritage Edition* of the Bible and sees all the people with black skins and kinky hair.
Moses, Noah, Abraham, Joseph, Melchizedek, Solomon,
David, Goliath, Job and his friends, the virtuous woman, Mary,
Elizabeth, the shepherds, the wise men, Herod, the ten virgins,
Nicodemus, the prodigal son, the good Samaritan, and Lazarus.
The twelve disciples all are black in this version of the Bible!

Before becoming too critical, our white brethren must examine much of the literature produced under their control. How

many different ethnic groups were depicted in their Sunday school and adult literature or Bibles? Who were those characters in modern pictures of the Last Supper? Is the Christ in the popular portraits the real Christ of the Scriptures? These pictures, which many have come to accept, are not accurate representations of the peoples of the Middle East where biblical history was lived.

The Bible is a multiracial book. Some assert that the real challenge is not to find people of color but rather to find whites in the Bible.

Commitment to biblical truth leads one to conclude that all humans came from one man, Adam. Therefore, blacks who have found a new sense of significance in either their African heritage and/or presence in the Scripture must be careful. One must be warned not to separate themselves from the human family. If any member of the human race digs deeply enough for his roots, he or she will be led back to Noah and his three sons. Further digging will lead us all to daddy Adam and the mother of all the living, Eve.

Biblical truth, contrary to popular desires, does not paint a proud and prestigious heritage for the human race. The Bible declares that Adam, though created in innocence and holiness, sinned against God. This act of disobedience plunged the entire human family into sin and death. Truly, sin is a genetically inherited trait within the human race. Regardless of one's color, gender, language, ethnic, national, educational or economic background, sin is present. Mankind's common ancestry has left us with a common problem – sin.

Biblical truth condemns rather than exalts sin. Our society seems to be on a suicide mission. We are that generation that calls evil what God says is good and good what God calls evil. This perverted perception affects perspectives on the race issue. Both blacks and whites argue their respective roles in his-

tory to demonstrate the superiority of their race rather than the
supremacy and mercy of God almighty.

Bold assertions based upon limited data may prove to be
intellectually embarrassing when further information is gathered. In the 1960s, James Cone, a prolific writer concerning the
oppression of blacks, built his argument around the Exodus
motif. The Exodus motif referred to God's deliverance of the
Jews from their bondage in Egypt. He developed his thinking
along the following lines. God is for the oppressed (Jews) and
against the oppressor (Egyptians). White people are oppressors
and black people are oppressed. Therefore, God is for the liberation of blacks from white oppression. In the theological
world this was called liberation theology. It drew very definite
racial lines.

Does such a system reflect a proper interpretation and application of the biblical text? Clearly it does not. The divine
deliverance had a divine purpose. The Israelites were to be the
people of God. They were to be in bondage to Him, not free to
do what they pleased.

Integrity would demand that oppressor be defined more as
a character trait than color-coded. Certainly one would not excuse the oppressive rule of Papa Doc Duvalier in Haiti or the
massive massacre that took place in Uganda simply because
these rulers were black! Not all oppressors are white, and not
all the oppressed are black.

Even more troubling for the race-based Exodus motif is the
new discoveries of blacks in the Bible. Many scholars maintain
that some of the ancient civilizations were ruled by people of
color. Yes, many, if not all, of the Egyptian Pharaohs are believed to have been black. If so, then, even in the Exodus motif,
the oppressor was black not white. Sin cannot be color-coded.

There is a debate today as to what color was Jesus. Blacks
argue that He was black. Whites argue that He was white, or at

least He was not black. Why is His color so important? Man is seeking personal status and pride. Christ is seeking humility and obedience. What difference does His color make when neither blacks nor whites are obeying Him? Jesus said, "Why call ye me Lord, Lord, and do not the things which I say?"

The challenge for every believer is to "Let God be true and every man a liar." Yes, the Bible has been misinterpreted and misapplied with the result being a misdirected Church. Prejudice among the people of God is one product of allowing culture to be imposed upon Scripture. Many people of color are still greatly offended by the injustices and oppression to which their fellow human beings have been subjected in the name of God. Today many people of color are being motivated to look at the Bible differently. God is not a racist.

The God who has revealed Himself in the Bible is no respecter of persons. His truth is the standard by which humanity and history are judged. No culture is to be imposed upon the Bible. Therefore, all mankind must diligently search the Bible to discover the mind of God. The historical grammatical approach to Scriptural interpretation is the only way to let God speak for Himself through His Word. Scripture is the final authority. Man's misinterpretations and misapplications of Scripture are to be corrected by sound interpretation, not by a denial of the trustworthiness of the text.

Chapter 3 –The Past That Plagues Us

Origin of Racism

It is difficult to identify the origin of racism. Certainly, the black man was held in high esteem in ancient history. The Bible contains references to their valor in battle, their attractiveness, their ability in business, their loyalty, and more. One scholar suggests that Moses' sister's problem with his marriage to the African woman was that she felt he was social climbing.

More and more scholars – white as well as black – are agreeing on the enormous contribution of blacks to the civilization and technology of the ancient world. There is growing evidence that Greece, the acknowledged mother of Western civilization and culture, owes a great debt to Egypt in many, many areas. An interesting point is that the benefactor Egypt was further indebted to Cushite/Ethiopian/Nubian blacks from the south of Egypt who ruled Egypt for an extended period of time. Joel Freeman and Don Griffin do a superb job of advancing this position in *Return to Glory: The Powerful Stirring of the Black Man.*

Apparently, racism was alive and well during the Middle Ages and following when European scholarship began to unearth and document the contribution of ancient peoples to modern civilization. Freeman and Griffin mention how the scholars deliberately Europeanized their discoveries, lest the African be cast in the light of having had intellectual, scientific, business, and navigational acumen that surpassed that of any other people of their generation and before.

Much of the evidence for the black man's contribution has been distorted deliberately. Fortunately, the serious researcher can find documentation of some of the dastardly deeds. For instance, Freeman and Griffin found that one of Napoleon's officers noted that the nose of the Great Sphinx was Negroid in appearance. He ordered his men to blast the nose off the Sphinx lest the world be made aware that the Egyptians had honored a black man by sculpting the face of the Sphinx with the stylized physical features of an African. The officer no doubt assumed that the ancient civilization which produced the colossal Sphinx was composed of people with similar features since that is the way great art is generally done.

The Biblical Concept of Race

Some definitions will be helpful for the following discussion. They are taken from *Webster's New World Dictionary* (Collins, 1979).

Race: Any of the varieties of mankind, mainly the Caucasoid, Mongoloid, and Negroid groups, distinguished by kind of hair, color of skin, etc.

Racial: Of a race, or ethnic group; of or between races.

Racialism: A doctrine, without scientific support, claiming the superiority of one race.

Racism: Same as racialism; the practice of racial discrimination, segregation, etc. based on racialism.

Origin of the Race – Evolutionary Model

In my five decades on this planet, I have learned that one of the deepest concerns of the human psyche is "Where did I come from?" Some adopted children, upon reaching adulthood if not before, have a desire to seek out their birth mothers. This is an elementary version of the debate that is overtly and covertly at the heart of much public discourse.

Constructive debate on the question does not seem to be possible because of the emotion with which some people approach the discussion. The evolutionary model of our origins has allowed the dispassionate killing of babies for 25 years. Now, certain groups and individuals have begun to target the elderly and people with special needs.

The evolutionary model also supports racism in the white supremacist argument that only whites came from Adam and Eve. They would have us believe that black people are other than human. This argument was widely held during the dark era of slavery in this country. I was a guest on a Christian radio talk show in Virginia. A white supremacist caller framed the question this way, "We know white people came from Adam. We do not know where black people come from. What does your guest have to say about that?" For some reason, the caller chose to speak to the host and not to me.

My response was: "The Bible is clear in Romans 5:12 that sin entered the world by one man and was passed to all his descendants. If only white people come from Adam, then only white people are sinners."

Not all people are logical. There are others who hold the caller's viewpoint. I have in my library a booklet that teaches that very point: Christ died only for the sin of Adam's race (that is, only for the sin of white people).

As is true of so many groups, Mormons have a rather elaborate concept of the origin and destiny of the black man.

Also true to the pattern of man-made religions, Mormonism is anything but static. Their former bedrock stand against inclusion of blacks in their church has been relaxed somewhat in the pluralistic environment of the eighties and nineties. Mormons now allow blacks to affiliate and to attain lower-level position in their ecclesiastical hierarchy. However, they still deny that blacks can attain the highest levels.

Not to be outdone, the Black Muslim sects, of which there are a number, have developed their own creative concept of the origin of humans. Black Muslims believe that Allah created the original man and woman as black persons and that Mr. Yacub, their name for the Devil, created the white man. It is rather common among individuals and groups that they react to a horrendous lie which puts them down, by adapting the lie so that it suits their purposes. Who can deny that the Black Muslim's lie sounds every bit as likely as the concepts advanced by the white supremacists and by the Mormons?

Biblical Model

The biblical model stands in stark contrast to other theories. According to God's Word, all people have a common ancestor, Adam. All people have a common problem, sin. All people have a common solution, Jesus Christ. Period. End of discussion.

Denial of Black Presence

The general populace tends to be unaware of the other sides of many problems. The race question is no exception, believe me. In the face of so much rhetoric about the negative origins of the black man, the masses supported all manners of injustice, beginning with slavery, but also including the systematic destruction of families, individuals, and their self-esteem. In the name of their god and his pick-and-choose doctrines, slavers and their cohorts used young black girls and women to sat-

isfy their fleshly lusts, while restraining evangelists and hu-
manitarians who desired to speak justice, mercy, and deliverance to the captives.

One must not overlook that the African chiefs were co-
conspirators in that dastardly enterprise. The selling of one's
brothers and enemies helped solved the slave traders' problem
of getting in and out of Africa alive with their human cargo. To
such ones, slave trading was undoubtedly not a personal matter. It was strictly business. The slavers of the Western Hemi-
sphere, however, invented their own rules to explain how they
could flee an oppressive governmental system and yet imple-
ment a system ten times as oppressive in the New World.

It is true in the annals of history that great men are created
in times of great need. The slave question precipitated the rise
of a number of giants on the world stage. We have but to recall
abolitionists such as Benjamin Lundy, William Lloyd Garrison,
Rev. Robert B. Hall, Theodore Weld, Levi Coffin, Charles G.
Finney, William Phillips, John Mason Peck, and Henry Ward
Beecher, to name just a few. There is no way to adequately as-
sess and honor the untold number of whites, Native Americans,
and blacks who maintained the metaphorical machinery known
as the Underground Railroad. Harriet Tubman (Grandma
Moses) receives a fair amount of publicity. But the success of
the Railroad was a direct result of the indispensable secrecy
which surrounded it, leaving us with a dearth of information on
this monumental effort.

Must Jesus Bear the Cross Alone?

Some contend that all the nations in Genesis 10 are Caucasoid. This is a result of the same worldview that classified
black people as subhuman. Today, many have difficulty com-
prehending how anyone could subscribe to both of the following statements:

All men are created equal and are endowed by their Creator with certain inalienable rights.
— Declaration of Independence

Article I, Section 2 of the Constitution of the United States counts blacks as 3/5 of a person for determining how many Representatives would be allotted to each state. (However, blacks could not vote for their Representatives.)
— From the Constitution of the United States

Worse than that, blacks did not count at all for social, humanitarian purposes. The mega-acre plantations of the South built an economy on forced labor. The magnificent ante-bellum homes that cover the South from Natchez to Mobile and from Augusta to El Paso bear mute testimony to the unwilling contribution of millions of black men, women, boys, and girls to the building of a nation. The planters justified their actions after working themselves up to view their slaves as chattel. The typical working class white person saw the slaves as persons who had taken their jobs away from them.

With a kind of situational logic, it is a small leap for those who want to believe that blacks were created inferior to read the Bible through glasses which see all Bible names as belonging to white folk. (Even blacks pick that up in school and in church, of all places.) Consequently, when the Bible refers to a patriarch or a matriarch, such adherents automatically assume the race of the person to be white.

It is fairly widely held that certain persons in the Bible were black, including the unnamed Ethiopian treasurer of Acts 8:26-39 and Paul's ministerial colleague, Symeon called Niger (Acts 13:1). Some others such as Simon of Cyrene, who carried the cross for Jesus, are more questionable. However, many persons who casually engage the Bible text treat all these persons as white.

Nor are Americans the sole users of this brand of convoluted logic. South Africa is reported to have four racial classifications. Their locally contrived hierarchical pecking order is white, Asian, colored (white-black mixed blood), and black. Apparently money can make up for one's "unfortunate accident of birth." Whereas most of the world, including Japan, would classify individuals of Japanese extraction as Asian, the South African system classifies such individuals as white because of their economic wealth. The absurdity of this position requires little exposition.

Fortunately, a growing number of black scholars and white scholars are calling this skewed worldview into question. The battle to turn the worldview right-side up is a difficult one, nonetheless. The upside-down view is held not only in many cases by the "man in the pew," but also by a large number of otherwise erudite scholars and pastors. This is due largely to the way that this tarnished worldview has permeated the writings and teachings of some Christian teachers.

McKissic and Evans, highly regarded African American ministers and theologians have done us a considerable service in assembling a large collection of mainstream evangelical thoughts on the subject. They quote Ramm (*The Christian View of Science and Scripture,* pages 336-337) as saying:

> *The Table of Nations gives no hint of any Negroid or Mongoloid peoples. . . . the effort to derive the races of the entire world from Noah's sons or the Table of Nations is not necessary from a biblical standpoint, nor possible from an anthropological one.* (page 18)

McKissic and Evans go on to cite the more logical point of view held by the *International Standard Bible Encyclopaedia* article on Ham:

Recent studies of African history reveal the existence in central Africa of a high level of civilization, probably nurtured by the posterity of Ham. (page 601)

On the other hand, the 1963 edition of *The Pictorial Bible Dictionary* failed to upgrade the general level of scholarship with its article on Ham:

(Ham) became the progenitor of the dark races; **not the Negroes** [emphasis added], *but the Egyptians, Ethiopians, Libyans and Canaanites.* (page 330)

T. Alton Bryant is another writer who squanders an opportunity to set the record straight. In *The New Compact Bible Dictionary*, the article on Ham likewise alleges that "Ham is the progenitor of the dark races, [but] **not the Negroes** [emphasis added]" (page 213).

McKissic and Evans note that Webster's dictionary boldly defines "Hamite" as "A Caucasian of the chief native race of North Africa." *The New Lexicon Webster's Dictionary* has the following definition:

Hamite – a member of a group of African people including the Berbers of north Africa, the Tuaregs of the Sudan, and the Galla of east Africa (after Ham, son of Noah).

Freeman and Griffin in their well-documented *Return to Glory: The Powerful Stirring of the Black Man* demonstrate how some scholars have gone to great lengths to rob blacks of their heritage. McKissic and Evans' monumental *Beyond Roots II: If Anybody Ask* (sic) *You Who I Am* contains numerous significant instances. In one case they cite from Dr. Clem Davies (*The Racial Streams of Mankind*):

The Hamitic stream is identified with the African, partly with the Indian, and partly with the Chinese. . . . **Ham was not a colored person.** *To begin with, the Egyptians were children of Ham, most of the Egyptians anyway;* **they were** *swarthy but not black.* . . . *Ham was the father of the Afri-can people and of the main body of the people of India.* . . . *Hamites are found today in the dark races of the world, the backward races. We speak of "darkest Africa," and it is "dark" in more senses than one, for it was in this section of the globe that the offspring of Ham have been most prolific* [emphasis added]. (page 19)

Curse of Ham

Keil and Delitzsch also discuss the so-called "Curse of Ham":

In the sin of Ham there lies the great stain of the whole Hamitic race, whose chief characteristic is sexual sin; and the curse which Noah pronounced upon this sin still rests upon the race. . . . *Although this curse was announced upon Canaan alone, the fact that Ham had no share in Noah's blessing, either for himself or his other sons was sufficient proof that his whole family was included by implication in the curse, even if it was to fall chiefly upon Canaan.* (pages 157-158)

McKissic and Evans found errors among ancient writings also. They quote the Hebrew-English edition of the *Babylonian Talmud*:

Our Rabbis taught: three copulated in the ark, and they were all punished – the dog, the raven, and Ham. The dog was doomed to be tied, the raven expectorates (his seed into his mate's mouth) and Ham was smitten in his skin. (page 21)

McKissic and Evans found a fanciful monologue in *The Bereshith Rabbah*:

The Rabbi Joseph imagined a conversation between Noah and Ham: "You have prevented me from doing something in the dark (co-habitation). (T)herefore your seed will be ugly and dark skinned." The descendants of Ham through Canaan have red eyes, because Ham looked upon the nakedness of his father; they have misshapen lips, because Ham spoke with his lips to his brothers about the unseemly condition of his father; they have twisted curly hair, because Ham turned and twisted his head around to see the nakedness of his father; and they go about naked, because Ham did not cover the nakedness of his father. (pages 21-22)

The Scofield Reference Bible (1917 edition, page 16) notes "A prophetic declaration is made that from Ham will descend an inferior and servile posterity." This error was corrected fifty years later without fanfare in the 1967 edition in a note on page 15.

Arthur Pink maintains, "The curse uttered by Noah did not fall directly on Ham but embraced all the descendants of Ham" (page 125).

The Old and New Hamitic View

In due time, questions began to be raised regarding the Noahic curse on Canaan. For instance, on page 53 of *Biblical Perspective on the Race Problem*, the following are asked:

1)   Against whom was the curse pronounced?
2)   Why was the curse pronounced?
3)   Was the curse legitimate?
4)   What was involved in the fulfillment of the curse?

The answers to the above questions show the utter absurdity of the concept of the "Curse of Ham." The problem is that too many people failed to ask these questions early on in the history of our country. And so slavery, Jim Crow, the Ku Klux Klan, the Aryan Nation, skinheads, and related aberrations flourished in one degree or another for hundreds of years; and even now they are with us.

Chapter 4 – The Present That Frustrates Us

The Importance of Crossing Ethnic Boundaries

The cultural face of the U.S.A. is changing rapidly. As we enter the new millenium, America is seeing immigration rates in unprecedented proportions. For more than 30 years, dissidents have been fleeing Cuba for our peaceful shores. Other oppressive regimes and poverty have contributed to the influx of new immigrants. Today, Miami has come to resemble a Latin American capital. Friends from Lithuania credit their coming to America to the fact that they "won the lottery," referring to the method by which permission to emigrate to the U.S. is rationed out in their country of origin.

A Rise in Cultural Pride

With increased multiculturalism, there has arisen a demand for cultural sensitivity. Culture may be defined as a group's agreed upon way of dealing with the world about them. Generally speaking, most cultural practices are neither right nor wrong. For instance, to Americans, driving on the left side of the road represents a difficult adjustment when we visit countries such as England. It is likewise difficult for the English to adjust to driving on the right side of the road when they visit our shores.

Some cultures used to engage in the reprehensible and morally wrong practice of infant sacrifice. Anthropologists surmise that this practice was a tool to control population growth. Now our country has approved 30 million abortions over the last 25 years. Sounds like the same thing.

There is a growing cultural polarization. People of different racial, ethnic, national, and gender backgrounds often look upon their differences as objects of superiority. Sometimes they look upon these differences as objects of scorn in others. We are experiencing an increase in cultural confrontations. As polarization increases, each intersection of two cultures provides an opportunity for friction. The media gives superficial treatment to the large incidences of crime within cultural groupings. But just let there be an altercation across group boundaries, and the media latches on like a hawk. This tends to help blow the matter out of its original proportion.

There is an assault upon Christianity as being an Eurocentric, white man's religion. It is interesting to read an unpublished defense of Christianity written by an Ojibwa friend entitled "The White Man's Religion." His audience consists of fellow Native Americans who feel oppressed by the white power structure. Such individuals are keen to identify the cause of their oppression. When they learn that the Christian message is liberation, they wonder why – after they have accepted Christ – they are still in bondage, especially to their white Christian brothers.

An interesting twist is that the preachers and missionaries of the Gospel allow themselves to be sometimes unwitting tools in the hands of those whose primary motivation is greed. The conquerors learned early that Christian people are less aggressive. Therefore, they were quite interested in allowing missionary activity to occur among conquered people.

A multicultural society is what many educators envision for a more tolerant U.S.A. Much is said of the small nations of Africa and Europe and how the citizens of necessity learn several languages in order to transact business on a daily basis. There is a greatly resisted move underway to adopt Spanish as the second language of the U.S. Employers are increasingly adding a diversity portfolio to the human resources department. Advertising is taking on a bold new look.

The Church must seek to fulfill the mandate of Matthew 28:18-20 within such cultural diversity. Culture is a mostly neutral artifact which can be either useful or a deterrent to communicating the Gospel. Fortunately, in *Communicating Christ Cross-Culturally* David J. Hesselgrave has spoken definitively to the considerations involved. Unfortunately, not enough missionaries, pastors, and lay persons in cross-cultural situations have read Hesselgrave.

But there are no excuses. The Great Commission did not say to make disciples *except* for those with cultural differences or *except* where you do not have cultural expertise. The command is to make disciples of all mankind.

The Church's Ministry Across Ethnic Boundaries

Clear communication of the Gospel requires an understanding of the culture into which the Gospel is to be communicated (1 Corinthians 9:18-23). When we think of the challenges involved in communicating Christ within one's native culture, think how much more awesome it is to communicate across cultural boundaries. Terms and issues need to be clearly defined and biblically critiqued (Proverbs 18:13; Hebrews 5:11-14).

The communicator needs to show profound respect for the host culture. This begins with a working understanding of the culture. My experience is that people are very forgiving and will make every effort to help communication happen for the person who is new to the culture. The host culture expects the novice to show reasonable progress in understanding over time.

Many churches are struggling with how to have an effective ministry in a changing neighborhood (Acts 10, 11, 15). My hat goes off to them. Ministry is often fraught with difficulty. But there are ways to get answers to perplexing questions. One cross-cultural church planter praises a soft-spoken community leader who was willing to take him under her wing during the formative stages of the church plant. Another church planter surrounded himself with local people for kicking ideas around before launching them. A national supervisor of church planters calls his team together quarterly for cross-fertilization and refreshment. What he has discovered is that there are few new things under the sun. Most of the problems faced by any given church planter have been dealt with successfully or unsuccessfully by others.

It can still be said, without refutation, that the most segregated hour in America is from 11:00 a.m. to 12 noon on Sundays, contrary to the Scripture (John 13:34-35; 1 John 3:16-19; 4:7-13). The proverbial visitor from Mars would marvel at this phenomenon. With all the great preaching that goes forth in America, how can it be that this obvious flaw exists and persists in the face of knowledge? (A related, encompassing biblical command that is being neglected is "Love thy neighbor as thyself.") One explanation is that our great teachers have only of late begun to make racial reconciliation a major theme. They have been led in this direction by Voice of Calvary Ministries, The Mendenhall Ministries, Voice of Biblical Reconciliation, and a handful of other groups. In recent years, national attention has been focused on the issue by the Promise Keepers movement.

Crying Needs

Answers to the accusation that Christianity is a white man's religion are needed (1 Peter 3:11-17, 15; Acts 6:10-8:1; 21:17-22:30). Bible scholars know better. But new converts and non-Christians tend to ask that question after they get to know that even some missionaries have practices that oppress and exclude persons. Mind you, those individuals who have been led to saving faith by the missionary/church planter reserve a warm spot in their hearts for the missionary. In their eyes, the missionary can do no wrong. The convert will defend the missionary's honor against all odds. Others in the target population are not inclined to be so understanding.

More contemporary expressions of the New Testament Church are desperately needed (Acts 6:1-7; 13:1; Ephesians 2:10-3:12; Revelation 7:9). The New Testament Church fellowshipped together, worshipped together, shared its resources with those in need, and even turned the distribution of aid over to representatives of the group which complained of being neglected (oppressed, if you will).

More models of the love of the brethren across ethnic lines are needed (John 13:34-35; 1 John 3:16-19; 4:7-13). One philosopher said he had nothing against Christianity; it was Christians he could not stand. So many of us bring shame on the name of Christ. Pricked in their consciences, a number of churches are active in inner-city ministries of feeding the poor and the homeless. True love asks "What can I do for and with the other person?" The answer is found in the modern proverb, "Give a man a fish and he will eat for a day. Teach a man to fish and he will eat for a lifetime." All through the Bible, God's people are told to empower the poor, the widow, the orphan, and the stranger. The greatest empowerment one can do is to point an individual to the Savior of our souls. It is surprising that after years of study and listening to sermons, many Christians conclude that John 3:16 encapsulates the entire Gospel and that the Gospel is limited to addressing the need of one's soul after death. To be with Jesus eternally is nothing to sneeze at. But it was Jesus Himself who stated His ministry as:

> *The Spirit of the Lord is upon me, because he hath anointed me to preach the gospel to the poor; he hath sent me to heal the brokenhearted, to preach deliverance to the captives, and recovering of sight to the blind, to set at liberty them that are bruised.*

> *To preach the acceptable year of the Lord* (Luke 4:18-19)

I don't know about you. But I claim all of that.

The inner city Church is rich in all the resources required for success in a capitalistic system, except for the entrepreneurial vision, management, and capital. Vision and management can be taught. But capital needs to be accumulated or borrowed. If the middle class Church would share its abundance of these resources, we could make a significant impact on poverty in our lifetimes. It seems to me that such radical thinking is required if we are to pursue that promise of Jesus, "Greater works than [mine] shall you do" (John 14:12). The Gospel of salvation must be accompanied by deeds of love (see 1 John 3:16-18; James 2:15-16). The positive witness of urban and suburban Christians together working out the Gospel as they address the needs (not necessarily the wants) of people everywhere will go a long way toward encouraging the addressing of moral and character needs (discipline, work ethic, family disintegration, etc.). Some of these concepts are caught better than they are taught.

There is a need for confession and correction of past misinterpretations and misapplications of certain texts in relation to certain ethnic groups and/or cultural preferences (Proverbs 18:19; 28:13; Acts 10:34-35; James 2:1-9). There must be an uncompromised and unashamed adherence to proper interpretation and obedience to the verbally inspired, inerrant Word of

God, the Holy Bible (Proverbs 23:23; Galatians 2; 3:27-29; Ephesians 4:1-7, 11-16).

Baptist Bible College of Indianapolis' mission is to glorify God by assisting local churches with affordable, accessible, quality higher education within a multicultural environment. We seek to be a model of racial reconciliation by operating with an integrated board of directors, employing staff from the various ethnic groups on an equal basis, and by encouraging students to enroll who likewise represent various ethnic groups. Our ultimate goal is to train Christian leaders to reach multi-ethnic urban America for Christ.

Chapter 5 – Crossing Ethnic Boundaries

Critical Issues in Racial Reconciliation

You may have heard the one-liner: For every extremely complex problem there is an equally simple solution – and it's always wrong. While I maintain that there is a simple solution to the problem of racial reconciliation, I have enough experience to realize that human nature will cause us to run into a lot of obstacles on the way to the solution, much as Israel spent 40 years traversing a distance of less than 200 miles as the crow flies.

In the first place, we must reject the wisdom of the world (Romans 12:1-2; James 3:13-18). At the same time, we need to acknowledge that the world, in general, has done a better job than the evangelical/fundamental Church in confronting the issues and in seeking to correct past errors. For example, the world generally takes strong action against people who make racist statements. Jimmy the Greek was fired for a comment he claimed was in jest. That would hardly ever happen in the church.

The world, however, fails to understand the bottom line issue. Their bottom line is the profit margin. Organized sports cannot afford to alienate the majority of its star players. The world's philosophy lacks moral wisdom and discernment. The solution to the world's problems and those of the Church requires that we receive God's wisdom (Proverbs 1:3-5, 7; 2:3-15; 3:3-4, 13-18; James 3:13-18). Make no mistake. You really have to go after wisdom; you have to *work* at it. It is not easy to find. Proverbs tells us that:

1. We must seek wisdom.
2. We must incline our ear toward wisdom.
3. We must receive wisdom.
4. We must keep wisdom.

Biblical wisdom is pure, peaceable, gentle, easy to be entreated, full of mercy and good fruit, without partiality, and without hypocrisy (James 3:17-18). Overtures toward reconciliation cannot always be taken at face value. We must understand the issue of control (Philippians 2:3).

When we begin reconciliation on a grand scale, some big questions need to be addressed. One biggie is: who writes the curriculum? The National Baptist Convention has 18.5 million members. They must be considered when talking about joint curriculum development. Care must be taken in selecting which principles to include and which to exclude from the discussion. Another item to consider includes the pride of the individuals and groups involved.

Who sets the standards for our reconciled relationship? A historic problem in our land has been the ignoring of people of color and an appalling lack of respect for the contribution of minorities to Christianity. The most effective tool for getting attention in the secular realm has been the economic boycott. Then all the capitalists want to get on the bandwagon. It would be more fun and more efficient if the Church could arrive at a workable resolution to important issues without the need to resort to power plays.

We will need to correct the pervasive lack of appreciation for the culture of others. This is nowhere more difficult than in worship styles, music styles, and standards of behavior in nonessentials. Some areas of difference are less important in their impact on both groups. Where the two groups' interests intersect, friction can be avoided by programming around the nonessentials. As an example of this, one care group leader began to assign generally late members to bring dessert instead of appetizers.

In our fundamental/evangelical churches, we find there are tests that people are required to pass in order to maintain fellowship: tests for the way we dress, whether and which movies people watch, clothing, hair style, even the use of the denominational name as part of the church's name. Many of these are good. Some come out of the culture which we create in our churches. But how many have love as a test of membership? Racial reconciliation and related items are often classified as political. Too often I hear the claim that the church's call is to "just preach the Gospel and not get involved in politics." Why is it that churches are willing to enforce standards that are carved around people's culture but we fail in the weightier matters of the Gospel?

We must understand the issue of inconsistency (Proverbs 11:1; 21:2-3; 24:23). God is calling for fairness in our dealings. The log in our eye is ever so conspicuous to a watching world, a world which is bravely trying to get its house in order in so many ways that they shame the Church.

Predominantly white schools will talk about the founding of America, a land where there is freedom to worship, freedom of association, and more. We go so far as to decry the practices of dead preachers and deacons. We confess and apologize for their sins. Love would require going another mile and welcoming into fellowship those for whom Christ died. There is little disagreement that slavery was unethical and immoral. Are we willing to plow new ground for the Lord? Our commitment to overseas mission is called into question every time one of the foreign nationals visits our churches and observes our lack of commitment to brotherhood at home.

Our talk often betrays our heart. For example, the descriptive language we use preaches volumes. In the news we hear violent white dissidents referred to as *urban terrorists* or *urban guerrillas*, while Rwandan dissident leaders are called *warlords*. Members of the majority group are said to have *killed* a large number of people, while Native Americans are said to have *massacred* a group of people. Other emotion-laden terms include *heathen*, *uncivilized*, and the like.

Be careful about offending others. Do not develop new rules when blacks come in. Some colleges require students to get a note from their parents before they may engage in interracial dating. In some circles, whites are allowed to say they don't like Jesse Jackson; but blacks cannot speak against Bob Jones University.

We must be biblical in dealing with sin. Sin is sin, no matter who commits it. At the same time, we must understand the issue of compassion (Acts 20:28; 1 Corinthians 12:12-14, 18-23, 25-27; Ephesians 4:11-16; 1 John 3:16-18; 4:7-12, 19-5:3).

Be aware of what our actions do to another's self-image. Through racism, some try to blot out positive role models in the other group. This suggests to the person's psyche that his group is less important, that they cannot do anything. Instead of tearing down another, we should be committed to building him or her up. Provide a measure of security in reconciled relationships. One brother mentioned that if someone was trying to lynch him, Jesse Jackson would make some noise. He was not so sure about what his white brothers would do.

Evangelical/fundamental blacks who graduate from majority seminaries have an expectation that they will find a place to serve the Lord in missions or in other forms of church leadership. Too often if a black person is saved, people in power will say he is called to black missions. We need to ask simply what does Jesus want? Service opportunities should be as broad as the Bible allows.

We must exercise critical thinking (Proverbs 21:3; 24:26; Philippians 1:9-11; Colossians 1:9-12). God hates pious people who put their own preferences ahead of doing the just thing. We need to avoid stereotyping. Just because we met one Klansman does not mean that everybody is one. We must deal with everyone individually. Similarly, we need to watch for extremes.

People need to watch their pride/anger. Many black brothers have been offended for so long that they are easily angered. We have to sift things through a biblical mold in order to gain the right understanding and to decide on a biblical course of action.

Seek to know the heart and head of the other person (Proverbs 4:23; 25:12; 27:5-6; 29:23-25; 31:9). If I understand the person, I know how to approach him or her. (See the earlier discussion on understanding persons in chapter 1.)

Since racial reconciliation may be a new thing for some readers, let me add how important it is to watch your communication. It has been quipped that everything we need to know we learned in kindergarten. Avoid name calling. Avoid talking down to people. Remember that as Christians, we do need one another. Our nonverbal cues speak louder than words. When a person of another color walks into your group, don't act like he doesn't belong. Don't slide over to keep from being close. People pick up when they are not wanted.

Seek to win individuals not races. We need to reach the one person God has placed in our lives. Individuals are different.

Perhaps the person whom we win may be used by God to win his or her entire group (John 4).

Chapter 6 – There Is Hope: The God Who Comforts

I will build my church....

– Matthew 28:20

The late sixties were a time of racial turmoil in American society. The battle for civil rights had intensified to a flash point. Many cities were literally in flames. Dr. Martin Luther King, Jr.'s voice had been silenced by a bullet from an assassin's rifle. Tempers were hot as America was challenged to live out the true meaning of its creed, that "all men are created equal."

Life in the Northeast was not as hostile for me. Although my high school was largely white, my experience was mostly positive. I can still remember being sent to the principal's office from my class early one afternoon. Upon entering his office the principal introduced me to a prospective high school teacher. "He has some questions about race relations at our school," the principal explained. "I thought you, as president of the student council, could best address some of his questions," he continued. Then the principal left the two of us in the room for a time of private conversation.

Martin Luther King's call for us to live together was a message of hope to me. Although his voice was silenced in 1968, I had heard another voice that same year – the voice of God communicated through the Bible. Two white men had come to my house and presented the Gospel of Jesus Christ to me. I believed on Christ, was baptized, and became the only black member of the church. Christianity proclaimed a brotherhood and promised a power that lifted the hope of racial reconciliation to a higher level than that promoted by King. The following Fall I enrolled at a predominantly white Bible college.

Three years later, while still a student, I was challenged, by chapel sermons and other students, to start an inner city church. The students desired more stability and structure than their weekly witnessing ministry on the city streets provided. The stability and structure envisioned was a church. I was the students' choice for leader and founding pastor.

Counsel concerning starting a new church was sought from various faculty members at the college. It was advised, among other things, that a mother church should be found. A mother church is a well established church that can offer credibility to a new ministry. New believers are baptized and become members of the mother church. After the new church establishes credibility in the community and formally organizes, its converts' memberships would be transferred from the mother church to the new ministry. This group of baptized believers would constitute the charter membership of the new church.

I began to inquire about possible interest of local churches to serve as a mother church for our new ministry. A meeting was arranged with a local pastor. The pastor was excited about partnering in such a ministry. He arranged a subsequent meeting between his church leadership and the leaders of the new church. Several white students and I met with the pastor and his leadership team.

The meeting began with great promise of a mutually beneficial partnership. There was a good exchange of ideas throughout. It was a very positive meeting until a church leader asked, "What kind of church are you planning to start?" Somewhat confused by the question, our simple response was, "We desire to have a church where the Gospel is preached and people are saved, baptized, and instructed from the Bible." The question was further clarified, "Are you seeking to start a black or a white church."

I burst out in laughter, then exclaimed, "If we are seeking to start a black church, we have a bad start because I am the only one in the group!" In a more controlled voice I stated, "This church is for anyone who repents of their sin and receives Christ as Savior and Lord. All who desire to live a life in submission to the Word of God are welcome, regardless of color." The meeting ended with cordial remarks and prayer.

A few days later, I received a phone call from the pastor. A meeting was arranged in the pastor's office. Upon entering his office, I noticed that he was visibly upset. Previously the pastor had been very enthusiastic about establishing a mother church relationship with the new work. He greatly anticipated renewed excitement being generated in his church due to their partnership in a local evangelistic effort.

The meeting was short. "I am afraid that I must inform you that, after our meeting, the men felt that your work is impractical. Therefore, they believe it would be fruitless for our church to give money to, or establish a relationship with, an impractical work." After a brief prayer, the meeting was over.

I was confused. A church for all believers who submitted to the lordship of Jesus Christ was impractical? The potential mother church was not willing to give birth to a mulatto (mixed, integrated) congregation. Practicality demanded an identity – a racially pure identity.

Our dream of a church for all people was characterized as youthful fantasy – not as hope inspired by biblical faith. Was such an assessment correct? Is a racially diverse church an impractical ministry? Must Christians be content with a segregated house? Must the hope of the Church as a model of a better way of race relations to a fractured society be sacrificed on the altar of practicality?

Before hope dies, let us take comfort from the fact that, whereas with men it may be impossible, with God all things are possible. It is comforting to remember that Jesus promised, "I will build my church and the gates of hell shall not prevail against it" (Matthew 16:18).

Christians can confidently work toward racial reconciliation within the Church because a multiethnic Church is the kind of Church which Christ is building. The Church is composed of believers, disciples. Christ is building His Church by saving people – people like you and me. We are Christ's personal possession. He purchased us with His own blood (Acts 10:28; 1 Peter 1:18-19).

The Church is pictured as an integral part of Christ himself. We are called the body of Christ (Romans 12:4-5; 1 Corinthians 6:15-18; 12:12-13; Colossians 1:24). Christ is the head of the Church which is His Body (Ephesians 1:22-23; Colossians 1:18). We are so precious and integral with Christ that to persecute a Christian is equated to persecuting Christ Himself (Acts 9:1-5).

Other biblical pictures display Christ's ownership and intimacy with us, the Church. We are the temple of God (1 Corinthians 3:16-17; 6:19-20; Ephesians 2:21-22). We are the bride of Christ (Ephesians 5:21-33). All of God's children should be encouraged by the biblical pictures of a people so intimately identified with Christ. This is the Church which He is building – a Church which consists of all believers, regardless of ethnic background, who are uniquely owned by and associated with Christ.

While the ultimate completion of the Church depends upon Christ, He has granted believers the privilege to participate as workers with Him in the building (Matthew 28:19-20; Ephesians 4:16). The Church will be completed, even though at times the workers may walk off the job or fail to follow the blueprints. Saints are commanded to participate in the building project. Jesus says, "Go ye, therefore, and teach all nations, baptizing them in the name of the Father, and the Son, and the Holy Ghost, teaching them to observe all things whatsoever I commanded you and, lo, I am with you always even to the end of the age" (Matthew 28:19-20). Here we have both a command to build and directives as to what to build.

The disciples are to come from "all nations," referring to all ethnic peoples. The Church that Christ is building does not consist of one ethnic group. Rather, the Church is composed of saved people from every ethnic group. We are responsible to proclaim the saving Gospel of Christ to all peoples within our community.

We have a debt to pay to all mankind, not just to our kind (Romans 1:14). How can the Church justify the mass exodus of churches from our cities when the racial makeup of the city began to change? People are born again by the incorruptible seed of the word of God (1 Peter 1:23). The removal of the impregnating seed, the Word of God, from a community is paramount to spiritual birth control. The declining birth rate of true disciples of Christ in our cities is devastating. The consequence of withholding the Word of God is the growing moral crisis within our cities. The Scriptures warn that, "Where *there is* no vision, the people perish: but he that keepeth the law, happy is he" (Proverbs 29:18). We know that people need to be saved. Yet how convicting is Romans 10:12-14:

For there is no difference between the Jew and the Greek: for the same Lord over all is rich unto all that call upon him. For whosoever shall call upon the name of the Lord shall be saved. How then shall they call on him in whom they have not believed? And how shall they believe in him of whom they have not heard? And how shall they hear without a preacher?

When the people of God fail in our responsibility to proclaim the Gospel to all people, how can we fulfill our duty to make disciples?

The watching world should be able to see within the family of God a reflection of the heart of Christ. The heart of Christ embraces all of us who believe on Him. Following salvation, the church is to baptize disciples, by means of water, and teach them the commands of Christ (Matthew 28:19-20). Identification with Christ and other believers is being spoken of here. Our identity in the community should be more as His disciples than in terms of our respective race. It was said of the early integrated church that "the disciples were called Christians first in Antioch" (Acts 11:26). Such a church is very practical.

Christ is building His Church, which is the family of God. Believers are to be co-workers with Christ in building the Church. The blueprint for the New Testament Church is ethnic inclusive.

Those who participate in Christ's program can take comfort. Our Lord promises, "And lo I am with you always, even to the end of the age" (Matthew 28:20). The Christ who died to purchase the Church – He who is personally building the Church, the One who gives the blueprints – is the Christ who promises His personal presence with those who participate in His plan for a multiethnic Church. All who are involved in racial reconciliation within the Christian Church should be comforted by the fact that Christ will build His Church in the hearts of men and women and the very gates of hell will not prevail against it.

Further encouragement comes from considering the oneness of the Church. The Scriptures teach that oneness in the body was the brainchild of God, created by the cross, and was a major issue in the New Testament Church. We shall explore this point at length later.

Oneness Is Biblical

Having departed from the biblical blueprint, many American churches are constructed according to cultural norms rather than congruent to the commands of Christ. The American culture of racism is well reflected in the American church. We, the Church, are still trying to live down the reputation that 11:00 a.m. Sunday is the most segregated hour in America. In relation to racial matters, there seems to be more world in the Church than Word in the world. The Church must give greater attention to its instruction manual, the Bible. Some Christians claim that racial reconciliation is cultural or political and not biblical.

It is resistance to this present cultural shift that blinds some to the biblical teaching on racial reconciliation. Some Christians justify segregated churches by claiming that racial reconciliation is the cry of a humanistic multicultural society. The Church is exhorted to resist the pressure of politically correct thinkers. This warning must not be discounted because of the existence of a worldly multicultural pluralism which lacks a moral basis.

The Church must be careful that – in rejecting worldly philosophies – we don't, inadvertently, reject biblical teaching. Reactionary theology often exposes error without explaining the biblical alternative. The lack of clear direction, and sometimes the presence of misdirection, in the Church with regard to racial reconciliation has resulted in a segregationist mentality in many believers.

The following illustrates how segregated our thinking has become. In the 1980s I called a meeting of black and white evangelical pastors to discuss the race issue. The challenge was given that we must stop talking about each other and start talking to one another. The emphasis was upon identifying the issues that divide the Church racially. Our purpose was to seek resolutions. There was a polite exchange of ideas.

When the meeting was finished and everyone else had left, an African American pastor had a few words of wisdom for me. This pastor had graduated from a predominantly white fundamental Bible college. At the time, I was ministering to a predominantly African American assembly, although we had some white members. The pastor expressed his encouragement concerning the meeting and then advised me, "Brother, you are doing a great work (ministering to African Americans). You are on the wall like Nehemiah. Do not come down to speak with these Sanballats and Tobiahs." (Reference was being made to the white pastors.)

This racially coded advice was meant to be an encouragement. Yet, Sanballat and Tobiah's suggestion to Nehemiah to come down to speak with them is demonstrative of the saved being distracted by the unsaved in building the Church. Furthermore, Sanballat and Tobiah desired to destroy the work of God rather than to build it up. There is no reference in Nehemiah 6 to Christians, black and white, seeking ways to unify in building the Church. Such racial segregation is more reflective of American culture than the teachings of the Bible.

Because of our unbiblical responses to injustices of the past, we justify unbiblical methodologies of church planting. This is not to say that every homogeneous church is unbiblical. It is to say that the widespread practice, and success, of planting homogeneous churches is more reflective of a culture of racism than obedient to the Christ of reconciliation.

Separate but Equal?

Racism created a separate and unequal society, a society of injustices and inequities which – while affecting all – had obvious social and legal abuses along color lines. Even today, studies continue to reveal large discrepancies in equity and justice in American society depending upon one's color. As a result, exterior pigmentation has become a color code for internal character. Superiority, oppression, power, anger, bitterness, distrust, and fear are deeply rooted in our culture. Security in American culture is not to be found in laws or institutions, no matter how noble these may be. Rather, it is color which comforts first. Thus, there is a more immediate feeling of security and comfort when an institution, even the church, is the right color.

The Church has been affected and is challenged by a color-coded society. "The only thing whites can do for me is give me their money and leave me alone," one African American leader said. Another African American pastor reportedly said, "No white preacher would ever stand in my pulpit."

An African American evangelist said that he shared the Gospel with a woman who wanted to know what color Jesus was. The evangelist inquired as to what difference would the color of Jesus make. The woman reportedly said, "If Jesus is white, I do not want to go to heaven!" These comments represent the challenge which many whites fear when they are urged to take the Gospel to all.

Some blacks would justify such reactions because of white racism. Douglas Blackmon's article in the Wall Street Journal contained a report which offers hope:

But the generation of pastors and deacons who at times physically barred the doors of lily-white churches against African Americans in the 1960s is passing away. Taking their place are forty-something church leaders energized by a new wave of conservative Christian evangelism, which seeks to win followers both from nonbelievers and from other branches of Christianity. For them, the impetus for eradicating race problems isn't politics. It is spreading their interpretation of the Gospel to anyone who will listen, black or white. (page A8)

The same Journal article also carried the story of the local black family of four whose funerals were held in a white church in their hometown:

... no black church was big enough to hold the anticipated [crowd] of mourners.

First [Southern] *Baptist Church stepped forward to help. ...more than 2,000 African Americans crowded the long wooden pews.....*

Anywhere else, such a trifling act of small-town goodwill might have been unremarkable. Here deep in the once-segregated South, however, it was one more manifestation of a profound and startling shift among the most conservative of religious believers. (page A1)

The culture has convinced some that they lack the responsibility and the power to make disciples from any ethnic group but their own. The homogenous church growth concept has been embraced by many. And it works! People like to be with others of their own kind. The definition of their own kind may be a common class, culture, or race.

Often in such settings, compassion – especially personal responsibility for the lost – becomes selective. There develops a spiritual blindness to the believers' responsibility to take the Gospel to people economically, culturally, and/or racially different from themselves – people whom God has sovereignly placed in their lives. While great efforts are taken to see that the Gospel goes across the sea, little or no effort is made to take the same Gospel across the street. These irresponsible actions too often are justified by stating that it is not one's responsibility to reach people with the Gospel who are of a different cultural and/or racial background. Historically, mission boards and other institutions recruited minorities, not as Christian leaders with a compassion for the world, but as specialists with a passion for a single group, their own.

These practices have assisted in creating great confusion. Some whites honestly question their ability to win any person of color to saving faith in Christ. Others simply state to African Americans, "I will never be as effective as you in reaching your people." The usual result of such thinking is that these believers make no attempt to make disciples of other ethnic groups. They have little or no sense of responsibility for their neighbors' eternal destiny. The church remains color-coded.

The color-coded church persists even at a time when the culture is undergoing unprecedented change. Many cultural voices are calling for a multicultural America. There is a cry for us all to just get along with each other. We are looking for institutions to reflect the ethnic diversity of the communities in which they exist. The laws of the land call for significant punishment for institutions which violate anti-discrimination laws.

It is understandable why the Church rejects the underlying philosophy of secular *multiculturalism* which denies absolute truth. Christians believe in absolute, exclusive truth. Objective, absolute truth is to be found in the Bible. The Church must expose the erroneous philosophies of the world. It must not be brought into conformity with the world. Rather, the Church must discern the mind of God from the Bible on any issue being discussed. Does the Bible have anything to say about ethnically inclusive churches? Is there a biblical multiculturalism, at least with respect to different ethnic peoples?

Oneness Is the Brainchild of God

The Bible does offer an alternative to secular multiculturalism. Oneness of different ethnic groups within the Church is the brainchild of God. Unity with diversity is biblical. This is the Church which Christ is building. Believers are called out of various ethnic/racial groups and united as one in Christ. This biblical concept of oneness is the brainchild of God.

First Person Plural

In Ephesians 1, Paul calls God blessed because He has:

- blessed **us** (vs. 3)
- chosen **us**, ...that **we** should be... (vs. 4)
- predestinated **us** (vs. 5)
- made **us** accepted (vs. 6)
- (given **us**) redemption (vs. 7)
- abounded toward **us** (vs. 8)
- made known unto **us**...(vs. 9)
- (given) **us** (vs. 11) ... (so) that **we** should be...(vs. 12).

Paul is extolling the Person (vs. 3), the will (vs. 5), and the grace (vs. 6) of God as manifested in His salvation of a multiethnic people. We know Paul is speaking of a multiethnic Church because he is a Jew writing to Gentiles (Ephesians 2:10-15). The unity of Jew and Gentile in Christ is the will of God (Ephesians 1:5).

The Church is composed of born-again believers from every ethnic background. The new birth is not accomplished by genetics, nor by the will of man, but by God (John 1:13). We have been made alive by God (Ephesians 2:1-5). God is our Father. If we have a problem with who is in the family, our problem is with the Father, not with the children. Like the elder brother in the prodigal son parable, too many of us don't like the way the Father treats those whom we consider to be prodigals (Luke 15:11-32). For some, merely being from a different ethnic background makes one a prodigal. We should thank God for the multiethnic family He has created.

God has communicated, by special revelation, that the New Testament Church was a multiethnic Church. Paul says that God made a mystery known to him by revelation (Ephesians 3:3). This mystery of Christ was not made known to previous generations (Ephesians 3:4-5). It was revealed by the Holy Spirit – not to secular humanistic multiculturalists – but to holy apostles and prophets (Ephesians 3:5). The mystery, which was conceived in the mind of God and revealed to the holy apostles and prophets, is that the Gentiles and Jews should be fellow heirs and of the same body (Ephesians 3:6).

Biblical racial reconciliation is primarily prophetically correct rather than politically correct. Wherever a political issue is biblical, it is correct. Therefore, racial reconciliation is both biblically and politically correct. Pauline ministry includes preaching the unsearchable riches of Christ and making all understand the mystery. Remember, the mystery is a racially united Church. A multiethnic Church is to be a testimony of the wisdom of God to heavenly observers (Ephesians 3:10). What message are these observers receiving as they gaze upon today's racially segregated church?

In summary, the ministry of racial reconciliation is the communication of a biblical mystery. The Church is responsible to model this biblical alternative to the secular pluralism of society. A successful ministry of racial reconciliation bears testimony to the wisdom of God. Racial reconciliation within the Church is biblical. Racial reconciliation in Christ is the brainchild of God. Furthermore, peace between the people of God is the creation of God.

Oneness Is Unity Created by God

More than being the brainchild of God, a reconciled body is the very creation of God. The biblical ministry of racial reconciliation is not a humanistic attempt to bring different racial groups together in the Church. Rather, it is living out the unity which God already established through the cross. One cannot proclaim the complete work of the cross without proclaiming that there is peace between Jews and Gentiles in Christ.

During the three decades of my Christian life, I have heard numerous sermons on the fact that believers have peace with God. Yes, we all were enemies of God and were reconciled to Him by the death of Christ (Romans 5:8-10). This reconciliation creates peace with God (Romans 5:1). The wrath of God has been appeased. Therefore, there is no condemnation to those who are in Christ Jesus (Romans 8:1)! Some discerning believers have noted that the use of 2 Corinthians 5:18 to support a ministry of racial reconciliation is a misapplication of this text. The reconciliation spoken of in 2 Corinthians 5:17-21 is reconciliation between man and God.

However, reconciliation between God and man is not the only peace spoken of in Scripture. My heart has often been comforted by sermons about the peace of God. When worship and prayer replace worry, then peace calms the heart and mind. Philippians 4:6-7 promises that the God of peace will literally guard our hearts and minds with a peace that passes all understanding through Christ Jesus. What a wonderful benefit for those who have believed on Christ! Yet, this peace, too, is between God and man, not man to man.

Peace with God and the peace of God are personal benefits which have been secured by the cross. Many believers have enjoyed these benefits while living in disharmony with other believers. This disharmony between believers is often not because of moral or doctrinal disagreement – but race. Social segregation along racial lines is preferred and practiced by some believers. The cross condemns such willful segregation (Ephesians 2:14-15).

Chapter 7 – There Is Hope: Part II

Social segregation along racial lines is the norm for the American church. Some church leaders support segregated churches on various grounds, such as:

- Spiritual unity does not negate social distinctions.
- Equality under the law does not demand integration.
- Blacks and whites prefer to be separate.
- Complete integration would make everyone the same.
- Integration would lead to interracial marriage, which is considered at worst to be sin and at best to be unwise.

These reasons are not exhaustive, but reflective of the thinking of some who purposefully practice social segregation in the church.

Yet, the Bible clearly teaches that Christ, from two (Jew and Gentile), has created one new man. The new man finds his identity in Christ. Therefore, believers are united in Christ. Social segregation was practiced in biblical times. Peter testifies that it was forbidden for a "Jew to keep company, or come unto one of another nation" (Acts 10:28). Paul was charged with polluting the temple because he had taken the Greek, Trophimus, into the temple (Acts 21:27-32). Such social segregation is very similar to the denial of Christians from different ethnic origins to fellowship with a church, attend a school, or serve in a Christian organization.

The abolishment of the middle wall of partition in the temple speaks precisely to the issue of social segregation. The wall separated the court of the Gentiles from the court of the Jews in the temple. Josephus, the historian, states that there was an inscription forbidding a Gentile from going into the court of the Jews (Ant. VIII. 3, 2). All such segregation was abolished by Christ. Furthermore, Christ created a unity and peace which has social implications (Ephesians 2:15). A. T. Robertson's *Word Pictures in the New Testament* makes this comment about Ephesians 2:15, "Christ is the peacemaker between men, nations, races, classes" (page 527). Willful, racially segregated churches deny the social implications of the cross. The cross is the key reconciling event both between man and God and between believers.

Christians partake of numerous personal benefits provided in the person and work of Christ. Christ sets the standards – not the culture. It was a racist culture that color-coded American society and the church. Black-white segregation in our churches is the fruit of the sinfulness of man. The church followed the culture not Christ.

Today the culture seeks to create a unity without Christ devoid of objective truth – a unity based upon human feelings and moral relativism – a unity secured by competition and demand. The world's fight for unity has resulted in racially divided armies prepared to attack their opponents, other racial groups. America is still polarized along racial lines.

The Church must reject the culture of the past and present. She must look to Christ for true reconciliation – a reconciliation that brings equality of privilege and responsibility. Christ has created this unity through the cross. It is a unity that transcends race and color. Furthermore, it is a unity that provides equal access into the very throne room of heaven.

Oneness is Equal Access to God
(Ephesians 2:17-18)

In Christ, both Jew and Gentile are reconciled into one new man. This new man is composed of believers who have equal access to the Father (Ephesians 2:17-18). Regardless of one's color, Christ opens the door of the throne room and invites all believers to commune with the Father. There are no race-coded glass ceilings in heaven.

The prayer life of some believers is affected by focusing on a segregated church rather than on the triumphant Christ. A black man explained to me that missionaries regularly discouraged his dreams that God could use him to do great things similar to those reported by the missionaries. He reasoned that if God answered the missionaries' prayers, certainly God could answer his prayers as well. Finally, his faith was encouraged by a black pastor who emphasized the greatness of our God rather than the greatness of our race. To date the man has a ministry of faith. He has seen God do great things. Thanks be unto God that when we pray there is not an angelic receptionist screening our prayers based upon the color of the saint. The password for entrance into the very presence of God is Jesus Christ!

Equal access carries with it great responsibility. Believers of color must stop sacrificing dreams on the altar of white supremacy. The ultimate progress of the Church is not stopped by whites. The excuse, "The white man would not let me do it," must be replaced with praise to the God who answers prayer. He has whatever we need to do the will of God.

Christians, black and white, need to be asking God for the spiritual, physical, and material resources to advance the kingdom of God. Unfortunately, we would rather compete with and blame each other. Yet, James 4:1-3 is very instructive at this point:

From whence come *wars and fightings among you?*
Come they *not hence,* even *of your lusts that war in your
members? Ye lust, and have not: ye kill, and desire to have,
and cannot obtain: ye fight and war, yet ye have not, because ye ask not. Ye ask, and receive not, because ye ask
amiss, that ye may consume* it *upon your lusts.*

Perhaps if the Church would pray as much as it debated and
competed, the cause of Christ would be better served by a racial reconciled community of believers – a community which
bears light in a darkened society.

American society is plagued with numerous problems, of
which racism is one. Equal access means that each believer has
the responsibility to believe God to work in his or her situation.
It is time to stop waiting on the government, the society, and
the *man!* The answer to America's problems is not in the White
House, the courthouse, or the schoolhouse. These institutions
need guidance from the God of righteousness. The answer to
America's problem is in God's house! The Church must offer a
biblical alternative to the moral relativism of the culture. We
must demonstrate that we are Christians by our love one for
another. For this, each of us is equally responsible to ask the
Father that we may receive.

Oneness Is Fellow Citizenship (Ephesians 2:19)

Patriotism is a good virtue. I am grateful to be an American. Although far from perfect, this country has much for
which one can be thankful. Even in relation to racial matters,
contrary to some critics, progress has been made. Consider the
number of black mayors and the rising black middle class. The
goal has not been reached, but positive steps have been taken.
The journey from slavery to segregation to discrimination to
civil rights should be noted. I, for one, do not plan to leave
America until I am relocated to my permanent home, heaven.

Believers need to remember that we have an eternal citizenship in another country. I was faced with a practical application of this truth in 1991. During Operation Desert Storm, American troops bombed Iraq. A co-worker and army chaplain was activated and sent to assist the troops. A fellow missionary and Iraqian by birth was visiting family in Baghdad when the conflict broke out. He was in Baghdad with his sickly mother throughout the entire conflict. In fact, his mother died before he escaped from Iraq.

During the Desert Storm conflict, I was reminded that I had fellow citizens both in America and in Iraq. Heavenly citizens are scattered throughout the world. Heaven will have representatives from every nation, kindred, language, and people (Revelation 7:9). Biblical racial reconciliation is, in part, a recognition of the fact that we are fellow citizens of heaven. The Church is called pilgrims and strangers on earth (1 Peter 2:11; Hebrews 11:13-16). Truly we seek a better country, heaven. We need to start preparing now for how life will be then. Heaven is not a segregated country. The church should not be a segregated assembly.

As believers, may we hold high the blood-stained banner of the cross. May our patriotism for heaven shine brighter than any earthly alliance. This is not to deny our duty to our country. It is to awaken us to an eternal perspective. May the watching world see, through our reconciliation, that we are fellow citizens of a better country.

Biblical reconciliation, oneness in Christ, creates a bond even greater than a common citizenship. We are family.

Oneness is Family Relationship (Ephesians 2:19c)

The oneness that God created in Christ grants believers equal access to God and makes us fellow citizens of heaven. These two, alone, should provide powerful motivation for racial reconciliation. Yet, the next two analogies in Ephesians 2 speak of such an intimate relationship that reconciliation cannot be logically denied.

Journalistic TV shows at time dramatize the reunion of a family whose members have been separated for years. Sometimes the separation was due to children being given up for adoption to different adoptive parents. Whatever the reason, the show focuses upon the search and discovery of the missing family member. Then the hour of reunion arrives. The cameras close in as two strangers embrace. A family is reunited!

This should be the response of the saints as we discover other believers – a family reunion. More often, rather than an embrace, we brace ourselves for conflict.

I was invited to speak at a predominantly white Christian university during black history month. The university plans culturally challenging chapels and events at this time each year. My assigned topic was "Black History Week in a White Christian University." The more I thought on the topic, the more I sensed the potential competition and conflict inherent in the title.

The day finally arrived. An intercultural student group conducted the chapel. When my time to speak arrived, I walked to the pulpit and stated my assigned topic but informed the audience that I was changing the topic. I explained that I felt that some students would be opposing the fact that every year this time the university brings in some minority speaker to push African American history at the student body. The topic which I felt more fitting for the occasion was, "Christian History in a Christian University." I informed the students that the study of history which deletes the identity and contributions of many of your family members leaves you short-changed. To discover that missing history is like a family reunion. Christian history is not color-coded. God has used, and continues to use, His people in history. We all need to rejoice at what God has done through the family.

Ephesians 2:19c states that in Christ, Jew and Gentile are members of the household of God. This means that we are family. Galatians 6:10 speaks of the household of faith. In 1 Timothy 5:8 the word is used in a context which clearly speaks of blood family relationships. Certainly families should be reconciled. Who wants to argue in favor of torn and divided families? The family of God should be reconciled across racial and color lines.

Family peace and unity are beneficial and beautiful. The family is the basic unit in society. Healthy family relationships contribute much to the development of mature children. Psalm 133:1 declares, "Behold, how good and how pleasant *it is* for brethren to dwell together in unity!" Racial Reconciliation is family business.

Scripture use of the family analogy to illustrate the unity of believers in Christ supports racial reconciliation. Family unity is beautiful. Yet, the final analogy transcends all others mentioned to this point.

Oneness is Common Habitation for God (Ephesians 2:20-22)

One of the great mysteries of Christianity is the fact that God Himself lives within the believer. "...Christ in you, the hope of glory" (Colossians 1:27) is a wonderful truth. This truth, which encourages personal significance, has racial reconciliation implications.

God not only indwells me but all other believers as well! In Ephesians 2:20-22 Paul uses the analogy of a holy temple being built for God to live in. Each believer is a part of this building. 1 Corinthians 3:16 and 1 Peter 2:5 use the same concept. Together the Church is being formed into a holy temple where Almighty God dwells.

Every Christian should desire to be in the presence of God. Since God indwells all believers, believers should, therefore, desire to be with other believers. When we are with believers we are in the presence of God. Yes, together we are the dwelling place of God. This is a profound analogy of the brotherhood of believers.

God has so constituted the Church that we need each other to provide the structure in which He has chosen to live. The Church is a living organism. Its life comes from the God who indwells it. Our growth is dependent upon our togetherness. Each one contributes to the building, but no one is independent (Ephesians 4:15-16). There exists a divinely instituted interdependency among the people of God.

Racial reconciliation reflects the fact that God dwells in a diverse community. The presence of God is to be found in all people who have trusted Christ for salvation. May a reconciled Church, with its splendid array of a rainbow of people of color, allow the brightness of His presence to capture the attention of our society. The temple in which God dwells transcends race.

Christ is building a Church composed of every ethnic people group. The concept of a diverse Church was the brainchild of God. The New Testament Church – according to revelation and constitution – is a reconciled body. Jew and Gentile have been made one in Christ. In Christ all believers have equal access to the Father, are fellow citizens of heaven, are family members, and are the dwelling place of God.

These analogies speak powerfully for racial reconciliation. Yet, one may ask if these are merely isolated Scriptures. Was diversity in the Church a major or minor theme? Several Scriptures illustrate that cultural/ethnic diversity was a major New Testament theme. However, it should be noted that the issues were not color-coded as is the case in America.

Chapter 8 – Oneness Is a Major New Testament Issue

The American church in the twentieth century struggles with the concept of racial reconciliation. Should racial reconciliation within the Church be a priority goal? The breakup of the family and fracturing of relationships, in general, are frustrating. Certainly, a call for reconciliation between differing people groups seems somewhat naïve in light of the present state of affairs. Some feel that the Church is too fragile to tackle racial reconciliation.

The realization that Christ is building the Church gives comfort. There is no enemy in heaven or hell that can destroy that which Christ is building. The Church which Christ is building is a multicultural/multiethnic Church. It is a Church in which Christ establishes an organic unity and peace between different ethnic peoples who believe upon Him. All who seek to team up with Christ in building the New Testament Church must at least acknowledge this fact. Reconciliation between believers is a major New Testament theme.

Not all in the Church embrace the concept that racial reconciliation is a major New Testament theme. In the sixties and seventies many church leaders resisted integration on the basis that it was a communist agenda or the social gospel. Still today, some Christian leaders believe the call for reconciliation to be an unbiblical, or minor, concern for the church.

One afternoon while sitting at my desk the phone rang. The secretary answered as usual. Soon my intercom buzzed, and I answered. The secretary told me that someone on the line was very upset. He had demanded to speak to someone in administration. I made the connection saying, "Hello." During the next several minutes I was allowed to speak only one sentence. The caller was a pastor from a Midwestern state. He was demanding to be taken off our mailing list. He was offended by the fact that our college newsletter promotes a racially diverse student body. He informed me that God was a segregationist. He concluded by speaking of racial reconciliation as "this thing (racial diversity) being promoted by the world, the ecumenical crowd, and now by Independent Baptists. I don't need this material coming to my desk!" After he hung up I instructed the secretary to honor his wish and remove him from the mailing list. One cannot help but wonder what this pastor preached to his people on Sundays concerning race relations.

Not all pastors who oppose a diverse church believe God to be a segregationist. Some simply do not believe racial reconciliation to be a major issue for the church. They acknowledge that it may have grave social and/or political implications; but feel it would be a distraction for the church to become involved. Race relations is not considered by them to be a major concern in the Bible.

Christians may debate the issue based upon human preferences and perspectives for ages. But to discover the mind of God concerning the Church, we must turn to the Bible itself. Paul gives sound advice in Romans 3:4, "...let God be true, but every man a liar...." What does the New Testament have to say about diversity and unity? Is it a major or minor issue?

The Gospels reveal that Christ crossed cultural and social barriers in His ministry. The great cultural divide in New Testament times involved Jews and Gentiles. The Jews were descendants of the Old Testament patriarch, Abraham. It was with them that God had established the covenants and given the law and the promises. The lineage of Christ, from the human side, was primarily Jewish (Romans 9:4-5). The Gentiles represented all other peoples. The Jews believed themselves to be better than others. They were proud of their religion, race, culture and tradition (Romans 2:17-20). Christ confronted them with a new perspective, a multiethnic perspective.

Jesus Confronts Cultural Assumptions

The heroes in Christ's stories often confront rather than confirm Jewish racial pride. Such is the case with the Good Samaritan. Although the Jews despised the Samaritans, Jesus portrays the Good Samaritan as a role model of loving one's neighbor (Luke 10:30-37).

Jesus also extols the faith of the centurion (Matthew 5:8-13). A centurion was a Roman officer with one hundred men under his command. The Jews were under the rule of Rome at this time. Christ presented multiethnic role models before a people who were ethnocentric in their thinking.

Likewise, Christ crossed social-cultural lines. He answered the request of the Syrophonecian woman (Mark 7:25-30). He talked to the Samaritan woman. He went into the town of Samaria and ministered to the people there (John 4).

Christ not only used multiethnic role models and crossed over social lines, He also taught and modeled multiethnic principles as well. He denounced the superior and self-righteous attitude of many of the Jewish religious leaders (Matthew 23:10). Their elevation of tradition to the level of truth was particularly offensive to Christ (Mark 7:1-13). Their equating racial heritage to spiritual inheritance was spiritually blinding and eternally damning.

Christ taught that the message of salvation was for a multi-ethnic people. He plainly stated that he came for more than just the Jewish people (John 10:16). He challenged his disciples to look on a people ready to receive Him. The people of whom he spoke were Samaritans. The Samaritans, in the thinking of most Jews, were not viable candidates for the kingdom message (John 4). The disciples, like many Christians today, would have reasoned that the Samaritans did not want their message. At least, the Samaritan would not receive the message from a Jew, would they? Yet, Christ saw them as people ready to receive Him.

The perfect model of cross-cultural evangelism is recorded in John 4. The statement, "He must needs go through Samaria," is instructive. Although looking at a map reveals that the most direct route between Judea and Galilee (John 4:3) was through Samaria, it was not culturally acceptable for a Jew to walk through Samaria. The Samaritans were of mixed blood, having been subjected to intermarriage during the captivity. Technically, therefore, they were not Jews. Apparently, the Jews considered that being chosen by God put them on a pedestal above everyone. They referred to the non-Jewish Gentiles as "dogs" and to the mixed-blood Samaritans as "despised." Jesus, in His typically loving way, did not rely on sermonizing about equality. He used His own actions as an object lesson. I can imagine Peter asking Him, "Why are you taking this highway. Don't you know that this road leads to Samaria?" The Bible simply records that the mission of Christ – to redeem a multiethnic people – necessitated that He "must needs" go through Samaria.

Isn't this true of us? Don't we need to be about our Father's business? What are some areas in our lives where we need to address issues of sin and compromise directly? The Bible is clear. 2 Corinthians 5 tells us in no uncertain terms that God our Father was in Christ reconciling the world to Himself. And

He has given to us the ministry of reconciliation. Cross-cultural evangelism requires living above prejudice for the sake of souls, for the sake of brotherhood, and for the sake of decency. Cultural prejudice blinded both the Jews and Samaritans. Prejudice had blinded the Samaritan woman to the preciousness of the Savior. She responded to the Son of God with the racially charged, "How is it thou, being a Jew, asketh drink of me, which am a woman of Samaria?" (John 4:9). Prejudice had clouded this woman's view of the Son of God. She initially saw him as a Jew. She represents many blacks today who refuse to listen to the only true Messiah because they perceive Him to be the white man's God. Please note that before the conversation ended the Samaritan woman saw Him as the Christ! (See John 4:25-30.) Christ had captured a prejudiced heart. Many need to be freed from the blindness of prejudice today. Truth frees one to behold the Lamb of God who takes away the sin of the world.

Likewise, prejudice today blinds some to the preciousness of souls, just as prejudice had blinded the disciples to the preciousness of a soul. When they observed Christ witnessing to the Samaritan woman they marveled that he talked with her (John 4:27). They were more concerned about the social implications of the conversation than the salvation of a soul. Their spiritual blindness is further amplified as Christ challenges them with the spiritual hunger of the people of Samaria (John 4:33-38). This popular missionary text is seldom applied as a challenge to believers to take the Gospel to a people group they dislike. The compassionate Christ pursued a people ethnically different from Himself and despised by His race.

Consistent with His teachings and model are Christ's final instructions to his disciples before his ascension into heaven. Remember His command in Matthew 28:19 was to "...teach all nations...." In Acts 1:8 He affirms that after the coming of the Holy Spirit the disciples would receive power and become His

witnesses in Jerusalem, Judea, Samaria, and to the entire world.
The expansion of the Gospel is to different ethnic people. Jerusalem and Judea represented the Jews. Samaria represented
Jews who had intermarried with the Assyrians. The entire
world represented all other peoples, Gentiles. The Spirit of God
would send the disciples of Christ to the peoples of the world
with the Gospel.

**The book of Acts records the spread of the Gospel to all
the people of the world.** Acts presents a survey of the formation of the New Testament church. The multicultural and multiethnic nature of the Church is obvious. The multicultural
nature is confronted immediately in Acts 2:1-11. Gathered at
Jerusalem were Jews from every nation (Acts 2:5). There was
ethnic unity. All were Jews, but there were differences in culture, nationality and primary language (Acts 2:6-11).

The cultural differences were magnified in Acts 6. The
church was charged with cultural bias. The charge centered
around the fact that one cultural group was receiving unjust
treatment. The Grecian Jews claimed their widows were being
overlooked by the Hebrew Jews in daily assistance given by
the church (Acts 6:1). The charge was one of favoritism in the
New Testament church! The apostles wisely directed the
church to deal with this matter (Acts 6:1-7). A possible church
split was avoided and the impact of the Gospel continued to
progress in the community.

The transition from cultural to ethnic diversity was initiated
by persecution (Acts 8:1). The text states that as a result of persecution, the saints – not the apostles – were scattered throughout the regions of Judea and Samaria. Those that were
dispersed preached the word (Acts 8:4). Philip had an especially successful ministry in Samaria (Acts 8:5-25). Philip is
also highlighted in his further multiethnic ministry of present-
ing Christ to the Ethiopian eunuch (Acts 8:26-40).

The fact that the Gospel was being preached to different ethnic groups created a challenge. Were these new Christians to be assimilated into the Jewish-Christian culture? Did maturity in the Christian faith demand the rejection of all Gentile heritage and culture? Should there be separate Jewish and Gentile churches? Could you blend differing ethnic and cultural people into one church? The New Testament church wrestled with all of these issues. Therefore, biblical data exists for our consideration as we seek to answer similar questions in the late twentieth century.

Peter becomes the point man for change in the church (Acts 10, 11). Peter is a key person in leading the church to accept the principle of unity with diversity. The Gospel bore fruit among a large number of Gentiles. Therefore, Christians of Jewish background needed to determine what standards must be obeyed to become a member in good standing of the New Testament church. Must Gentile converts obey the Jewish ceremonial laws? Did not obedience to these laws characterize clean people (those who are right with God), whereas disobedience characterized unclean people (those who are not right with God)? After all, Christianity originated with the Jews. They were the chosen people of God. Gentiles must be assimilated into Jewish culture, it would seem, in order to be acceptable to God. Certainly, God would want uniformity in the Church. Peter's experience, however, testifies to the opposite.

Perspective

Perspective often must be changed for one to have an effective ministry among people ethnically different from oneself. Acts 10 and 11 present a historical account of how God orchestrated a meeting between two men, Peter and Cornelius, that would change the perspective of the Church concerning multiethnic ministry. Both men were stretched beyond their cultural comfort zones in obedience to God. It was obedience to God which caused both of them to cross the cultural and traditional barriers which had characterized their religious faiths for decades. Social segregation in the name of religious/ethnic faith was challenged. The will of God for the New Testament Church was revealed to be multiethnic.

The Jewish Christians' concept of social uniformity was about to be adjusted. The New Testament Church would be one of unity with diversity. The process of change is pictured first through the personal journeys of Peter and Cornelius. We start with Peter who was a strong biblical leader. He was one of the twelve disciples, one of the inner circle members who shared private conversations with Christ, and a chief apostle. Yet, Peter was a racist. He had respect of persons when it came to Gentiles. Social segregation was a way of life for Peter. God was about to change his perspective.

One day at midday, as was his routine, Peter went to pray. This prayer meeting was unlike any of Peter's prior meetings. This was a prayer meeting where God wanted to speak to His servant rather than listen to him. Therefore, God put Peter into a trance and caused him to become hungry. Women have known for a long time that the best way to a man's heart is through his stomach. While Peter was hungry God began to communicate through a multimedia production. The text says a sheet was let down from heaven containing all manner of food. It was like a heavenly all-you-can-eat buffet loaded with all the good stuff, including pork and other meats which were unclean by Jewish dietary laws. Stomach growling and eyes glancing over the heavenly smorgasbord, Peter heard the divine invitation, "Rise, Peter; kill and eat" (Acts 10:13). Certainly, it was chow time. Peter was hungry. God had prepared the table with a large variety of meat. God had given the invitation to eat! One would expect Peter to eagerly rise and eat. Yet, the text says that Peter's response was an alarming, "Not so, Lord!" How could this man of God disobey a direct command of God?

Peter's response was a revelation of his character. He was a man of convictions. The problem with the heavenly table was that many of the foods had been declared unclean by God, and the Jews were forbidden to eat them (Leviticus 11). This was part of the Old Testament ceremonial regulations. Peter's refusal to eat demonstrated that he was more committed to obedience to the revealed word of God than personal pleasure. Peter was more a man of conviction than convenience.

The Church has had its share of Peters – Christians who hold to racial segregation because they believe it is taught in the Bible. Such individuals are not easily persuaded on issues by culture and political trends. They, like Peter, have convictions and will not change for expediency alone. Yes, a person can be godly and still have the wrong perspective on racial reconciliation. This will become more evident as God continues to bring Peter to a new perspective.

Christ-honoring convictions need to be based upon a comprehensive understanding of the Bible. But the real issue concerns how many times God must speak to His servant before he changes his convictions. God – not culture, not legislation – commanded Peter three times to eat. In each instance, the man of God said "No." Peter awakened from the trance still hungry but culturally clean. He was culturally clean but mentally troubled as to the meaning of the vision (Act 10:17). The heavenly table had not helped his stomach, but it had engaged his mind. The text says, "Peter doubted in himself what this vision which he had seen should mean." Biblical change begins with an honest examination of the whole counsel of God. The entire teaching of the Bible needs to be examined on any given issue to discern the mind of God.

Peter's concept of the New Testament Church was about to change. He was about to learn that the New Testament Church is larger than his cultural concepts of social cleanness. His change would not be motivated by either a political or a cultural agenda but rather by the word of God. Divine revelation would produce a change in Peter's convictions.

The real issue behind the heavenly vision of unclean foods was Peter's cultural bias against Gentiles. The text explains that while Peter was thinking on these things, men – having been sent by their leader, Cornelius – arrived and requested that Peter return with them to their master's home. Because of the vision and a word from God, Peter agreed to go with them. The next day they arrived at Cornelius' home. Peter asked why he had been requested to come. Cornelius explained that he wanted to hear the Word of God (Acts 10:32-33).

Cornelius gathered his entire family together to hear Peter's message. Peter preached the Gospel, and Cornelius' entire family was saved (Acts 10:24, 33, 44-48). What a miraculous act of God! Any salvation is a miracle of God. But even more astounding is that here we have Peter, a Jew, preaching in the home of Cornelius, a Gentile.

Peter, the man of conviction, had been changed. This change was evident by Peter's actions and words. When he entered Cornelius' house, Cornelius "fell down at his feet, and worshipped *him*" (Acts 10:25). Peter immediately had Cornelius stand and said, "I, myself, also am a man" (Acts 10:26). Peter began his address to the Gentile audience with the following confession:

> ... *ye know how that it is an unlawful thing for a man that is a Jew to keep company, or come unto one of another nation; **but God has shewed me that I should not call any man common or unclean*** [emphasis added]. (Acts 10:28)

Peter's perspective of Gentiles had been radically altered. Exactly when his perspective changed, the text does not state. But it took place sometime after the vision and before the men arrived. Immediately after the vision, he was not sure of its meaning (Acts 10:17). But by the time Cornelius' men arrived,

Peter responded to their request based upon his change of perspective concerning what was acceptable social behavior with Gentiles (Acts 10:28-29). The Old Testament laws of uncleanness had been changed by divine revelation. Peter's change of perspective is further confirmed by his statement. After Cornelius said that he sent for Peter to hear from him the word of God, Peter responded, "**Of a truth I perceive that God is no respecter of persons** [emphasis added]" (Acts 10:34).

God had changed Peter and effectively used him in a cross-racial ministry. However, the message which had been so vividly communicated to Peter was not the position of the early church which consisted primarily of converted Jews. Peter's new convictions would not be accepted lightly by concerned leaders of the church.

Sure enough, Peter's new convictions were challenged by the other apostles and brethren in Jerusalem. The joy of Gentile conversions was over-shadowed by the fact that Peter had crossed sacred cultural barriers. He had violated the social segregation code (Acts 11:1-3). The church demanded an answer for such behavior. Peter answered them by relating the entire story of the vision, his initial response not to eat, the men coming to take him to Cornelius' house, God's command to go, his obedience, his preaching in Cornelius' house, and God's granting to Cornelius' household the gift of the Holy Spirit (Acts 11:4-15). Peter concluded his defense by stating that, after that the Gentiles received the Holy Spirit as the Jews had at the beginning (at Pentecost) (Acts 2), he remembered the words of Christ, who had said, "John indeed baptized with water; but ye shall be baptized with the Holy Ghost" (Acts 11:16). Peter's final appeal was, "Forasmuch then as God gave them the like gift as He *did* unto us, who believed on the Lord Jesus Christ; **what was I, that I could withstand God** [emphasis added]?" (Acts 11:17)

Peter was a man of conviction, not of convenience. His convictions would yield to the authority of Scripture. Therefore, when he received a better understanding of the Scriptures, he changed his convictions to be in harmony with God. He stood by his new convictions even when challenged by leaders of the church. The church (who charged Peter with disobedience to biblical standards) listened to his defense. After hearing his case they, too, discerned that God had used Peter as a change agent. God, Himself, had granted repentance unto life to the Gentiles (Acts 11:18). God generally transfers truth to the Church through individuals who will submit to the authority of Scripture – individuals who esteem truth higher than tradition.

Cornelius' conversion introduced a new perspective into the Church, but the implications were yet to be realized. Gentile converts became much more than a small minority. Largely due to the missionary work of the Apostle Paul, Gentiles became a significance group in the New Testament church. The issue of universal church standards became a major concern. Christians of Jewish background may have accepted the fact that salvation was granted to the Gentiles (Acts 11:18), but many still believed that Jewish standards were the norm for the church. The issue of church standards was the focal point of a major church conflict (Acts 15:1-2, 5-7) – a conflict that ultimately required apostolic input for final resolution.

The apostles resolved the matter of universal standards in a way that acknowledged the multicultural nature of the Church. First, it was conceded that conformity to the ceremonial laws (for example, circumcision) was not necessary for salvation (Acts 15:1-19). Second, minimal standards were required of Gentile believers (Acts 15:20, 28-29). Third, the standards that were set acknowledged sensitivity to both Jewish and Gentile cultures (Acts 15:20-21). This was done that the Gospel might be most effective in a multicultural environment. Fourth, the

Christian leadership of Jewish background assumed the responsibility of communicating to the Gentiles their conclusion (Acts 15:22-29). This was particularly important due to the fact that Jews had demanded of the Gentiles uniformity to their standards (Acts 15:1-2, 5, 24).

The New Testament church was a racially inclusive church. Further affirmation is given to the inclusive nature of the family of God in that inclusive issues were major themes of the New Testament letters. The book of Romans addresses both Jewish and Gentile believers. Chapters 1-4 demonstrate that both Jews and Gentiles are sinners. The different lines of argument acknowledge different cultural backgrounds. In these chapters, Paul argues for common guilt both from a Gentile (chapter 1) and from a Jewish (chapters 2 and 3) perspective. Making cultural adjustments to communicate the Gospel clearly seems to have been an evangelistic principle for Paul (1 Corinthians 9:19-23).

Cultures may differ, but there are absolutes. The God of Scripture is God both of the circumcision, Jews, and of the uncircumcision, Gentiles (Romans 3:29-30). Christ is presented as the common cure for mankind's sinful condition. He is the only savior for both Jew and Gentile (Romans 3:23-26; 4:9-17). The fact that there are absolutes is of critical importance in a pluralistic culture that proclaims that all religions are of equal value. The one thing that is intolerable in our tolerant culture is exclusive statements. In this culture, Christians must affirm that Jesus is the way, the truth, and the life; no man comes to the Father but by Him (John 14:6)! We, as Christians, can not sacrifice the eternal destiny of people on the altar of temporal peace.

Other Scriptures speak to the issue of differences within the Christian community. Romans 14 and 15 give principles for inclusive relationships in a culturally diverse congregation.

Ephesians 1-4 and Galatians address the oneness of Jewish and Gentile believers.

1 Corinthians has much to say about unity with diversity as well. Chapter 3 calls for unity between factions within the Church. Chapters 11-14 call for a team perspective in the use of differing gifts within the body. While this does not speak directly to the issue of racial diversity, there are some sound principles concerning unity with diversity versus uniformity. Chapters 8-10 deal specifically with how to handle cultural differences within the Church.

Colossians 1-3 speak to the issue of cultural differences, too. The pastoral epistles are not silent on the subject of diversity, either. 1 Timothy 1 and 4 address some of the issues with which the multiracial church at Ephesus was wrestling. Paul instructs Timothy on how the saints should behave themselves in the church, the house of God (1 Timothy 3:15-16).

Titus 1:10-16; 3:8-9; 1 Peter 2:1-12 and Revelation 5:9; 7:9 all testify to the fact that the New Testament church is a beautiful rainbow of peoples who have been born into the family of God.

Oneness in the body of Christ is not a minor or peripheral issue. Rather, this is a major New Testament theme. Christ both modeled and taught the concept of a multiracial rather than a homogeneous church. In harmony with His model and in obedience to His command, the disciples of Christ built a racially diverse church. Many of the New Testament books record for us how the church sought to maintain unity with diversity.

Practical Oneness Demands Love At Its Peak

The Scriptural testimony is clear concerning the nature of the New Testament church. The Church should be, according to Scripture, a visible testimony of God's wisdom in making of two (Jew and Gentile) one new man in Christ. This should be a comfort to saints as they seek to unify around a standard higher than race.

The truth is that many saints find little comfort from the Scriptural teaching. At heart, they are pragmatists. They demand to see a model. On numerous occasions, I have expounded the Scriptures related to race relations before a Church body. Usually after I finish preaching, there are two questions I am asked. The first question is, "Do you really believe what you just taught." I answer this question by affirming my belief that the Bible contains the very words of God. To deny the Scripture is to call God a liar! The second question is, "Do you know anywhere this (blacks and whites worshipping together in the same church) is working?" Although models are few, there are some. However, the greater issue is the unbelief, disillusionment, and disappointment which often lies behind the questions.

It is a fact that healthy relationships are difficult to maintain even in homogenous communities. Divorce and lawsuit statistics testify to the fact that Americans have difficulty getting along with one another. Interpersonal relationships is a major problem among Christians, too. The introduction of another potentially problematic relationship (different races) into the church may seem destined to failure, a failure which may occur regardless of the fact that such a church is thoroughly committed to racial reconciliation.

Pessimism concerning the success of racially diverse congregation is not without reason. *Breaking Down Walls* recounts the death of a vision. Glenn, a Christian of Anglo-Saxon heritage, had a strong desire to work in a black community and become an agent of change in race relations. His optimism for change was greatly heightened by his introduction to Circle Church. He recalls:

The first Sunday Lonni and I visited Circle Church on Chicago's West Side, we felt like two parched, desert travelers who had finally crawled to an opulent oasis. On that Easter Sunday in 1971, the members were signing a "Declaration of the Open Church," Circle's vision of different races and classes coming together, not to assimilate into the culture of the majority, but to appreciate and celebrate in Christian harmony their differences in culture, class and race. (Washington & Kehrein, page 74)

Glenn states that Circle was "populated mainly by highly educated young adults – about 15 percent black, 5 percent Asian, and the rest white" (page 74).

This vision was never fulfilled. Circle Church cracked along racial lines. Glenn remembers,

I can hardly describe the pain I felt as the dream crumbled around our feet. As a high profile church, often pointed to by homogeneous church growth critics, the humiliation was publicly reported in Christianity Today *magazine. It was like watching a loved one die an agonizing, public death.* (page 80)

The dream of a multiracial ministry model had proven to be a nightmare. Such an experience could easily cause one to rethink the biblical teaching of racial diversity in the Church. However, although Glenn's faith was challenged it was not destroyed.

Since the failure of Circle Church, Glenn teamed up with Raleigh Washington, a black pastor. Together they have formed a partnership between two inner city ministries to provide a holistic ministry that unites faith and works: Rock of Our Salvation Church, a multiracial ministry, and Circle Urban Ministries, a Christian multifaceted community development program.

Biblical theology should never be abandoned because of human failure to live it. It is better to examine ourselves for the cause of defeat and seek God's wisdom for the way of success. Both Glenn and Raleigh believe that committed relationships are a critical foundation for multiracial ministry. Glenn sees this as a missing ingredient in the Circle Church collapse. He reflects:

> *Even now as I look back at the situation, I don't know what else could have happened because of the ominous breakdown in relationships. ... The time to install fire extinguishers is not while the house is burning. We learned the hard lesson that the time to work out racial differences is not in the middle of conflict. In a cross-cultural tinderbox setting, we have to be building relationships and working on the issues of trust, sincerity, and openness – key principles of reconciliation – all the way along. If relational depth is not there, a crisis will only expose it and cause everyone to retrench to their most defendable positions: blacks mistrusting whites and whites mistrusting blacks.* (page 80)

In *Breaking Down Walls* Raleigh and Glenn list eight critical principles for successful cross cultural ministry which does more than give lip service to unity with diversity: commitment to relationships; intentionality; sincerity; sensitivity; interdependency; sacrifice; empowerment; and call.

2 Peter 1:5-7 gives another eight principles for developing committed relationships: faith, virtue, knowledge, temperance, patience, godliness, brotherly kindness, and love. These principles begin with faith and lead us to the peak of human relationships, Christian love. In the context, these principles are related to the believer's growing in his or her relationship with God the Father (2 Peter 1:2). Growing in our knowledge of God can be related to growing in our knowledge of fellow believers.

Assurance concerning the attainability of committed relationships resides in the power and promises of God. His power
has already provided us everything we need for spiritual life
and godliness (2 Peter 1:3). The provision is secured through a
knowledge of God and His promises (2 Peter 1:3-4). It is
through these promises that we become sharers in the divine
nature (2 Peter 1:4). As we will see later, the ultimate expression
of the divine nature is love. God's love, in contrast to man's
love, sacrifices for the good of another rather than seeking self-
fulfillment at the expense of another. Man's lust, which is often
mistaken for love, is the source of much of the interpersonal
conflicts in the world today (James 4:1-2; 2 Peter 1:4).

Divine love is a critical building block in committed relationships. 2 Peter 1:5-7 reveals the process truth takes to free us
from selfish desires that we might share the selfless love of
Christ. If the Church is to move forward as a cohesive body
across racial lines, we must be freed to love. Divine love is the
glue which holds the Body together. The development of love
in the heart of a saint is a process.

The process begins with faith. This faith rests upon the firm
foundation of both the Person and promises of God (2 Peter
1:1-4). Therefore, in context the believer has sound doctrinal
reasons to expect to develop a committed relationship with
God. Likewise, there are sound theological reasons to pursue
interracial relationships. The Bible teaches that God has made
us, Christians, one in the family of God. Being a child of God
takes precedence over one's particular racial heritage or background (John 17:11, 21, 22; Ephesians 2:11-15; 1 Corinthians
12:13). Cross-cultural relationship is a family affair.

Faith rooted in sound doctrine is a good beginning. But
theory must be translated into action. Truth is not only to be
believed; it is to transform the believer. Therefore, Peter exhorts that virtue be added to one's faith. Virtue means "moral
excellence." At this point, a Christian decides to experientially

live out the relationship which God has provided and promised. Personal possession of the promised knowledge of the Holy One becomes an intentional pursuit. It is biblical to pursue cross-racial relationships. The Church needs to commit herself to manifest the fruit of faith, a variety of colors and cultures. We must dare to dream of a Church reflecting the beauty of a well-planned and cultivated flower garden. However, for the dream to become reality we must be willing to plant, water, fertilize, and weed. There needs to be dedication to transcend racial barriers through Christ (James 2:1-3, 8-9; Acts 10:9-34; Galatians 2:11-14; Ephesians 4:3).

Building solid relationships demands more than the dedication to do whatever it takes. Action that will achieve the desired goal needs to be based upon accurate Knowledge. True fellowship with the God of Scripture is not developed through feelings, human philosophies, or traditions, but by precise discernment of His self-disclosure in the Bible (1 John 1:1-10; 5:20-21). To know God is to know His word. One must spend time with Him, listening to Him (2 Timothy 2:15-16).

Interracial relationships require knowledge between people. Many saints do not know a single Christian from a race different than their own. We must study the Scriptures on the subject of healthy fellowship between saints. We must begin to discuss the issues of reconciliation with one another and seek wise counsel (Acts 10:9-34; 11:1-18; James 3:13-18).

Time spent studying the heritage and values of another people or group different from our own is a good investment. Generally, people enjoy talking about themselves to someone they trust. Therefore, book knowledge should be supplemented by personal interchange. This needs to be done one person at a time. The realistic goal is to win an individual not win a race.

Knowledge for academic purposes only will not help people bond. Movement from casual, superficial acquaintances to intimate trusting friendships requires the application of knowledge. Consistent application demands *Temperance*. Once certain principles and practices become clear, we need the self-discipline to obey those things which will help to build our relationship (James 2:19-25; Psalm 1). Temperance often means stopping actions we naturally do and creating new habits which minister grace to others. A few examples may include use of ethnic jokes, offensive symbols, demeaning language, patronizing actions and a lack of quality time commitments. Deep bonding does not occur quickly nor without investment. Having many shallow friendships is a testimony to one's lack of temperance.

Race fatigue may tempt a self-controlled person to become weary in well doing. However, tough and lasting friendships come with time. Patience in doing right produces a seasoned relationship with God. A friend once commented that in his observation, older Christians were either grateful or grouchy. Talking with them revealed that each person had experienced similar things throughout life. The difference was in their response to life's trials. The grouchy had refused to see things from God's perspective and had become complainers. They did not persevere in doing right. The grateful had patiently sought God's wisdom and grace through trials. They had grown to know and love God more even through difficulties.

We must understand that good, healthy, loving interracial/intercultural relationships will not flourish overnight. A white brother commented to me that he was tired of talking about race. My response was, "I'm tired of living with racism." The great divide did not occur overnight. Healthy integration will not be achieved overnight, either. We need to patiently continue doing that which we know to be right (James 1:2-12; 5:7-12). Strong relationships require long-term nurturing. We will reap in time if we do not faint.

The fruit of obedience is godliness. It is encouraging when faith begins to see truth transform relationships. Paul speaks of trials developing patience which develops experience which develops hope which in turn makes one not ashamed because the love of God is shed abroad in our hearts (Romans 5:3-5). There seems to be a new appreciation for the character of God through this process of growth. In a similar manner, the one who patiently does right discerns more about God's faithfulness and places greater worth in God's person and promises.

Pragmatic unbelief becomes personal praise of God as testimonies are established. When one begins to see the fruit of obedience, one begins to worship God because of God's worth. The discovery of another saint who shares your convictions regarding the Scriptures on racial reconciliation inspires your faith in the Word of God. To be led by God to groups of people who believe like you is extremely exhilarating! There comes a renewed sense of being like God, leading one to proclaim with confidence that God is present in the reconciliation movement.

Godliness speaks of a new compatibility. In regard to our relationship with God, it means that we have changed. We see better the value of the divine perspective. This compatible relationship is called brotherly kindness.

Groups founded on brotherly kindness among Christians may be seen as cliques. Relationships are formed around a sense of togetherness because of common goals, rejoicing together in victories and weeping together in defeats (Romans 1:7-12; Philippians 1:3-8; 2:1-18). Many saints would probably consider reaching this stage in relationships to be heaven on earth. Yet the text challenges us to a higher level.

The ultimate mark of maturity in a reconciler's life is Love. This love is more characteristic of the divine nature than brotherly kindness. This love does not wait for compatibility but seeks the good of the one loved at great personal sacrifice (1 John 4:9-19).

Love motivates us to seek reconciliation. It will compel us to reach out to all, seeking nothing in return. We have a compassion for the racist, the prejudiced, the perplexed, the protective, and the positioned. (See below.) Any sacrifice Christ asks of us for the sake of the kingdom is joyfully given. The desire is to help, heal and bless those whose lives are impoverished to the degree they are ignorant of loving God and their neighbor.

This text, 2 Peter 1:5-7, communicates a process of personal maturity from faith to *agape* love. Although this is a gradual process of growth, it is achievable by every believer (2 Peter 1:1-4). For those who are developing through this process, there is a promise of fruitfulness. "If these things possess, control you, they will make you that you will neither be idle nor unfruitful in the knowledge of Jesus Christ" (2 Peter 1:8). The immediate context speaks of an intimate and strong relationship with God. These principles offer great hope in the racial reconciliation struggle. Solid cross-cultural friendships must be built on sound doctrine and held together by love.

The subject of racial reconciliation stirs many emotions and responses. Some are plagued by past injustices. The growing diversity of America and the church's limited supply of successful models of multiracial churches frustrate others. Still others are terrified at the thought of further racial polarization and possible race wars in the future.

Comfort comes from the fact that God is in control. Hope for the future brightens when we consider that Christ has promised to build His Church and that the gates of hell will not prevail against it. Further, the Church that Christ is building is a multiracial Church. This was the goal and teaching of the apostles. Unity with diversity is a major New Testament theme. Critical to such ministries are committed relationships built on sound doctrine and glued together by divine love. In fact the color of Christianity is love.

Chapter 9 – Color Me Love

And now abideth faith, hope, love, these three, but the greatest of these is love.

– 1 Corinthians 13

Christians Are Commanded To Love

The racial turbulence of the sixties was not as trying for me personally as for many. I enjoyed a mostly comfortable and accepting environment in my largely white public school with all-white teachers. I served on the student council as a freshman, class president as a sophomore, vice president of the student council as a junior, and student council president during my senior year.

I was confronted with more racial tensions after being saved while a senior and entering the predominantly white fundamental/evangelical Christian community than from the non-Christians with whom I interacted. While God used many of my white brothers and sisters to minister to me in ways for which I will be eternally grateful, the fact remains that race became more of an issue after I entered the Church than it had been during high school. At first, I assumed that saints who had been believers longer than I, would have good Scriptural reasons for attitudes and beliefs which I witnessed and heard. An explanation was needed as I interacted with black friends whom I had invited to church activities in hope that they, too, would trust Christ for their eternal salvation. The seriousness of the race issue to the evangelization of people, especially blacks, became a growing concern for me.

Rejections, put downs, and misunderstandings based purely upon one's race can be very painful. Racism within the church made an unforgettable impression upon me as a young adult attending a fundamental Bible college.

I recall a story that is relevant at this juncture. One afternoon the phone rang. I picked up the phone and responded with the usual, "Hello." The voice on the other end generated a new excitement when I recognized it was Larry! Larry was a high school friend I had not seen for a couple of years. However, the joy which his voice had initially stirred in my soul was quickly overwhelmed with sorrow by the message he shared. "Charlie, have you heard the news?"

"No," I replied.

"It's sad, man. Jon is dead," Larry spoke slowly, seeking to hold back the emotions. At age nineteen, Jon, another high school friend was dead. He had been released from prison only thirteen days prior to his death. In that brief time, he had married and a domestic argument had ended in a fatal gunshot wound!

"O God! Why did it end this way for Jon?" My mind began to race back over the years of friendship I had shared with Jon. I remembered the night when, with tears in his eyes, Jon had walked the aisle to receive Christ after hearing the Gospel at a youth camp. Times when we went to church, prayed, and studied the Bible together all flashed through my mind. Jon had even talked strongly about attending the same Christian college which I attended.

But it was never to be! Why? Within the Christian community, racism in its subtle manifestations created a major stumbling block for Jon. I remember the drive home one evening after a youth rally. The preacher had given a dynamic and dogmatic presentation of the Gospel. I wanted to personally confront some of my unsaved passengers with their need to receive Christ. I prayed for courage. Finally, I asked, "Well, what did you think about the message?" All chatter stopped and a frightening silence filled the car for about thirty seconds, which seemed like an eternity.

"How could he say that?" responded an emotionally charged voice.

I sat for a moment seeking to discern the motivation for the objection – antagonism against morality, hatred of Christ, or arrogance? Finally, with a determination to take a stand for Christ, I asked, "How could he say what?"

"How could he tell us not to go to a secular college when up until a few years ago they wouldn't even accept us in their colleges?" my friend responded with strong emotion.

The response was both surprising and disarming! The preacher did have high praises for Christian colleges and harsh criticism for secular universities, but the major thrust of his message was salvation. But what do you say to your "brethren according to the flesh" to convince them that the Christ of Christianity really loves them when some Christians have historically rejected them?

One of the blacks in the car that night was Jon. Jon faced further rejection during a youth activity. The director took him aside and warned him not to get too close to the white girls. Jon was an outstanding high school athlete and a young Christian. He was not pursuing girls. They were seeking to be in his presence.

Some find answers to such dilemmas and keep moving forward; Jon did not. His inner conflict created fertile ground for black power advocates to plant seeds of destruction in his mind. He decided to attend a secular college, rather than a Christian college, in part due to a lack of Christian love by the church. He followed the wrong path to his death. But I will never forget that his course was changed in part due to his confrontation with racism in the church. What might his end have been if the love of Christ would have embraced him through the arms of the saints?

In the sixties, there seemed to be precious few who were willing to discuss racism within fundamental/evangelical circles. Sermons and counsel often criticized black leaders and excused and/or covered poor racial attitudes and policies/actions practiced by white believers.

While at Bible college, I began to study what God had to say on this subject. Early in my education, I wrote a paper entitled, "Prejudice and the People of God." This paper was written in part to clarify for myself what God had to say about racial reconciliation and to speak up on behalf of Jon. I sensed a responsibility to attempt to protect others from unbiblical barriers which leave persons feeling unwanted in the family of God.

Biblical love is commanded and should be an identifying trait of Christians. Every believer needs to discover and demonstrate love in relationships. The very life of another may depend on our love. Our color, black or white, has been sovereignly given without our choice; but we are commanded to love. Love is a choice. Lack of love is disobedience.

Love is given a high priority in Scripture. When asked what is the greatest commandment, Jesus declared love to be the greatest commandment. He named two objects of love – God and our neighbor. Furthermore, Christ made the assessment that love is the summation of the law and prophets (Matthew

22:36-40). Scripture declares love to be the goal of the commandments (1 Timothy 1:5); more preeminent than gifts (1 Corinthians 13:1-6); that which will last (1 Corinthians 13:13); an identifying mark of a disciple of Christ (John 13:35); and one of the attributes of God (1 John 4:16).

There are three aspects of biblical love which I believe have direct application to racial reconciliation within the Body of Christ. Since the Scriptures state that God is love and that anyone who knows Him will love his brother, it may be helpful to consider the three aspects of God's love for us. The challenge and responsibility will be for us to love others as God loves us (1 John 4:7-11). God loved us first, most, and with an open invitation.

God manifested His love toward us by devising a plan to restore our relationship with Him before we were desirous or deserving of such a relationship (Romans 5:8; Ephesians 2:1-5). Given the history of our country, the present polarization of racial groups, and the tension generated by a discussion of racial reconciliation, many prefer not to discuss the issue. But God's love moved Him to seek and work out a plan of reconciliation with us while we were still hostile toward Him (Romans 5:6-10).

The issue concerning whose responsibility it is to seek reconciliation first has a simple answer. Whoever desires to be like God will seek out reconciliation rather than waiting on the other side. True biblical reconcilers are mature saints. They reflect a growing conformity to the character and will of God. It is a compliment to be known as one who loved first, especially those of an ethnic group different than one's own.

A second aspect of God's love is that He loved us most. One of the challenges of multiracial relationships is the enormous cost. We may be misunderstood, falsely accused or rejected, and may even lose financial support. Yet God's love for us was manifested by humility and death (John 3:16 and Philippians 2:8). We who would be channels of His love to others must be willing to pay the price. Whatever the cost to us, it will be insignificant when compared to the price He paid to establish a relationship with us.

The third aspect of God's love is that it is an open invitation. God gave His Son that whosoever believes in Him might not perish but have everlasting life. The invitation is not limited by class, sex, race, age, or any other characteristic. Christians are to communicate the singular Gospel to the multiple ethnic groups throughout the world (John 3:16 and Romans 10:11-14). All who believe upon Christ have been redeemed by the blood of Christ and are members of the family of God (Ephesians 2:11-22; 4:1-6; 1 John 4:11). Saints should be sowing seeds of love as we obey and imitate God Who by His very nature is love.

Love the Lord With All Thy Heart, Soul, Mind

The Christian must see in God more than a command and example when it comes to love. God is both the motivation and source of Christian love. Our reluctance to pursue meaningful relationships with believers of different ethnic origins than ourselves is more of a reflection of a lack of appreciation for God's love than anything else.

Christ simplifies the law and the prophets into one command, "Thou shalt love...." First, our love is to be directed toward God and, secondly, toward our neighbor (Matthew 22:35-40). This twofold division is seen in the Ten Commandments. Love for God is addressed in Exodus 20:3-11, and love for neighbor in Exodus 20:12-17. Likewise, Paul declares that love for one's neighbor fulfills the second half of the Ten Commandments (Romans 13:8-10; Galatians 5:14).

Before we can properly love our brother, we must love God and be secure in His love for us. Love for God takes precedence over love for neighbor for good reasons. Our love for God is really a reflection of and response to His love for us. Christian love originates with God. We are expected to love because of our relationship with God, Who is love. Christ's command to love (John 15:12) reveals the source of love and its flow to the saints. This love does not spring forth from the goodness of man. In John 15:9, Christ states, "As the Father hath loved me, so have I loved you: continue ye in my love." Note that this love was modeled first by the Father's love of Christ then, secondly, by Christ's love for the disciples. This love is to be reproduced by the disciples' love for one another. The Holy Spirit produces such love in the life of a yielded believer (Galatians 5:22).

Our love for others in the family of God is to be an expression, through a yielded believer, of God's love for them. We are free to express such love because of our security in God's love. We receive God's love before we demonstrate it (1 John 4:10, 19).

Those who are most secure are least selfish. The world emphasizes self-esteem. The saint's self-esteem is rooted in the love of God. Those who are motivated by a need to earn or demand respect are self-focused. Love is other-focused. The significance of a saint is to be found in the praise of God rather than man.

Here is a starter list of facts saints should consider for a proper sense of worth. Man's being created in God's image:

1. Is the basis of our significance (Genesis 1:26-27).
2. Is the basis of capital punishment (Genesis 9:6).
3. Means that God provides protection for the poor (Proverbs 14:31; 17:5; 22:2).
4. Indicates that we are fearfully and wonderfully made (Psalm 139:13-18).

5. Is a sign of significance because the Creator has chosen to communicate with us (Psalm 19:1-8; 2 Timothy 3:16-17).
6. Shows that man is loved by God (John 3:16).
7. Shows that Christ identified Himself with mankind (Hebrews 2:14-17).
8. Is a reason that saints are objects of Christ's death (Hebrews 2:14-17; John 3:16; Philippians 2:7-8).
9. Is a reason that saints are justified by the resurrection of Christ (Romans 4:25; 1 Thessalonians 4:16-17).
10. Is why saints have access to God (Ephesians 2:18).
11. Is why saints are citizens of heaven (Ephesians 2:19).
12. Is why saints are members of the family of God (Ephesians 2:19).
13. Is why saints are the temple of God (Ephesians 2:22).
14. Is why saints are heirs of God (Romans 8:17).
15. Is why saints are joint heirs with Christ (Romans 8:17).
16. Is why saints are being changed into the image of Christ (Romans 8:29; 1 Corinthians 15:49; 2 Corinthians 3:18; Colossians 3:10).
17. Is why saints are being interceded for by Christ (Romans 8:34).
18. Is why saints have an advocate in Christ (1 John 2:1).
19. Is why saints are members of the Body of Christ (1 Corinthians 6:15-16).
20. Is why saints have been blessed with every spiritual blessing (Ephesians 1:3).
21. Is why saints are more than conquerors through Christ's love (Romans 8:37-39; 2 Peter 1:4).

These truths attest to the saint's significance to God. Believing the testimony of God should free saints from the pursuit of arrogance, attempting to prove themselves better than others. Racial superiority arguments among a fallen race are foolish. The Gospel message exalts God's love and mercy, not sinful man. If we are to boast, let it be in the Lord (1 Corinthians 1:26-31; Galatians 6:12-15). Those who recognize the greatness of their sin respond with great love to the Savior who forgave them (Luke 7:36-47).

Recognition of God's love and mercy should cause saints to conclude that relinquishment of their lives to God is a wise investment (Romans 12:1-2). Security in God's love lifts a saint from a victim to a victor mentality (Romans 8:31-39). Racism, with all of its dehumanizing effects, need not destroy the spirit of saints secure in Christ's love. Saints must begin to love others just as God has loved them.

Christians Are To Be Known by Their Love

A teenager, who had recently trusted Christ came to a weekly Bible study more animated than usual. He could not wait to share with me the fact that several people on the streets had commented that he looked like Jesus! Unfortunately, the resemblance was based upon the popular 1940 Warner Sallman's portrait of a blond, fair-skinned portrait of the head of Christ. We do not know the actual physical features of Christ. It is a fact that his ethnic origin was Jewish. Sallman's portrait, while popular and well done, is nonetheless a myth.

Christians have created a variety of images and positions to distinguish us from the world. From the fish, to the cross, to dress codes, to abstaining from certain worldly practices, to denominational names, to political and social positions Christians have sought to establish identifying marks.

Universal symbols and standards in an age of diversity are difficult to establish. The complexity of the issue is manifested in portraits of Christ. In a December 25, 1997, Indianapolis Star article entitled "The Many Faces of Jesus," staff writer Judith Cebula observes:

If it were simple to image Jesus the Divine, perhaps there would be only one picture of Him – the ultimate im-

age. Instead, Christians of every time and ethnic heritage have created their own....

For centuries, artists have created images of Christ to reflect their own cultures. European Christian art has dominated for 1,000 years, spreading around the world the idea that Jesus was white. Cebula continues:

...Sallman's Jesus has become controversial – an image that dominated American Christianity and reflected only its Caucasian experience. During the 1960s, artists began reacting to it, creating Christ as black, Hispanic and Asian American....

These newer images of Jesus have often made political, social, and theological statements about Christ and His followers. Perhaps our difficulty in creating a universal symbol is due, in part, to seeking cultural and temporal symbols. We need a standard that transcends cultural and temporal confinement.

The Scriptures offer a more culturally and temporal transcendent identifying mark for Christians – love. Christ clearly considers love to be a birthmark of His disciples. In John 13:35 He says, "By this shall all men know that ye are my disciples, if ye have love one to another." The Apostle John argues that love of the brethren assures us that we have been saved (1 John 3:14; 4:7-8). John further asserts that if one truly loves God, then he should love his brother as well (1 John 4:20-21.) The apostle Paul considers love the highest of Christian virtues (Ephesians 5:1-2; Colossians 3:14). Likewise, the Apostle Peter places love high among the Christian virtues (1 Peter 1:22; 4:8; 2 Peter 1:7).

It seems like God has joined truth and love in holy matrimony. Fundamental/evangelical believers have emphasized truth, often to the neglect of love. Yet, the Scriptures commonly speak of truth/faith/belief in a couplet with love as identifying marks of true believers (compare Ephesians 1:15;

Colossians 1:4; 1 Thessalonians 1:3; 2 Thessalonians 1:3; Philemon 5; 1 Peter 1:21-22; 2 John 4-6). The Christian's identity should be deeper than skin color, more intimate than necklaces, chains, bracelets, and pins, and more adaptable than cultural mores. Love provides a more significant identity than these because love is the very nature of God (1 John 4:8, 16). Therefore, to love is to be like God. When people behold our love they are to see a reflection of God. Thus Christianity is more an identification with an attribute of God than human symbols and cultures.

A friend of mine gave me a tee shirt with these words on the front, "It's not a black thing or a white thing." On the back are the words, "It's a Jesus thing." How appropriate that our Christian identity be rooted in Christ! It is time for Christians to show their true colors. Color me Love. As a saint, my true color is love. May a watching world see our color as clearly as it is communicated in the Bible.

Christian Love – Some Components

Love is clearly enjoined upon Christians by the Scriptures. Simply stated, love originates in God and is a reflection of the character of God. Saints secure in God's love are free to love God and others. Love of others is critical in a multiethnic environment. Yet, love is seldom defined. Is it merely a warm feeling? Is it popular opinion? Is it equal acceptance of all people and moral standards? Does the Bible give any objective standards by which our love may be tested?

The Bible does speak to the issue of love. Contrary to many popular views of a romanticized feeling-oriented, dependent concept of love, the Bible presents love as actions, motivated often by self-sacrificing concern for others based upon facts. The supreme motivation for racial reconciliation is love. Since we have been redeemed, we need the continual renewing of our minds in order that we might re-channel our energies, attitudes, action, and so forth according to the Word of God.

Jesus identifies love by obedience to the commandments which it prompts (John 14:15, 21; 15:10). Paul affirms the fact that love expresses itself in obedience to God's moral code (Romans 13:8-10). Love takes the lead in pursuing reconciliation, even at great personal cost (John 3:16; 1 John 4:10-11). Love is a choice to set our affections on eternal things and a commitment to move beyond mere words (1 John 2:15-17; 1 John 3:18). Love is action – moral action. Reconciliation is a moral issue (1 John 5:1-3).

Love is produced in the yielded obedient believer by the Holy Spirit (Galatians 5:22). In the context of 1 Corinthians 13, love is presented as the only true motivation for the use of various spiritual gifts in the Church. Through the principles listed earlier in this chapter, love will be presented as the biblical motivation to direct one's emotions, attitudes, actions, and will toward one's fellow Christian (especially with regard to interracial relationships). God, in His sovereignty, has made of two (Jew and Gentile) one new man (the Church) in order that by the enablement of the Holy Spirit we might minister to one another out of love. This is growing together in the knowledge of God and one another.

Those committed to building strong cross-cultural relationships can find profound instructions from the love chapter, 1 Corinthians 13. The church at Corinth was characterized by divisions and contention (1 Corinthians 3:3-4). Disputes and confusion concerning spiritual gifts deserved proper biblical explanation (1 Corinthians 12:1-3). Some believe that education alone will solve racial divisions and understanding. While education is important, Paul says that love offers a more excellent way toward reconciliation (1 Corinthians 12:31).

The more excellent way, love, places a higher priority on relationships than on personal performance. Communication without love becomes cold and irritating to your fellow saints (1 Corinthians 13:1). Professional success without love doesn't benefit your relationship with your fellow saints (1 Corinthians 13:2). Self-sacrifice without love profits your relationship nothing (1 Corinthians 13:3). Love is not just giving someone something – whether speech, gifts, or materials. Reconciliation demands that you give yourself.

Biblical love is the cement which is in the one loving and accepts the one loved as he or she is – and from this root relationship seeks to build the one loved into that which is best for him or her. What is best for another is determined by Scripture. Again, love is other-person oriented. 1 Corinthians 13:4-7 develops this thought.

"Love suffereth long" or is long tempered, patient (13:4). There are a few Scriptural illustrations of the use of this word that might help us to better understand its meaning. Matthew 18:26-29 is the parable of God's patience with us and an exhortation for us, therefore, to be patient with others. In James 5:7 we are to wait for the coming of the Lord as a farmer waits for his crops. Hebrews 6:15 speaks of Abraham's patience for God's promise.

These Scriptures should encourage us to be patient in our attempt to cultivate good interracial relationships. None of us is perfect. All of us need to invest with the understanding that it might not be until the next generation before the fruit of reconciliation is realized.

"Love is kind", or is tender, gracious, gentle according to verse four. We need to treat individuals, even those different from us, with gentleness. Love looks for ways to improve and bring out the best in others. Words, as well as actions, can be harsh and cold. Saints should treat each other with the respect due a child of the living God. Difficult relationships, as cross-racial relations often are, demand that one submit to God and ask Him for wisdom from above (James 3:14-18).

"Love envieth not" (1 Corinthians 13:4). This is the negative of to be jealous. Vine's *Expository Dictionary* makes the following clarification, "Envy desires to deprive another of what he has, jealousy desires to have the same or the same sort of thing for itself." In Acts 7:9, envy is used to describe that which motivated Joseph's brothers who sold him into slavery. Saints must be careful not to allow envy to lead them into tearing one another down. Black and white Christians are not meant to be in competition but rather to complement one another in advancing the kingdom of God.

"Love vaunteth not itself" (13:4). Vaunteth means to boast oneself, brag. Love is not anxious to "show off." Too often we are motivated by self-advancement rather than by concern for others. The self-absorbed mentality which characterizes so many of our generation must not dominate the Church. Race relations rooted in self-exaltation inevitably lead to a debate as to which group is better. A lack of love results in a lack of bonding.

"Love is not puffed up" according to verse four. Puffed up means to blow up, inflate. It is used metaphorically in the New Testament in the sense of being puffed up with pride (1 Corinthians 4:6, 18; 5:2; 8:1). Mythological beliefs of racial superiority cause people to lose touch with reality. Loving relationships must be built upon truthful relationships. Saints should let God work through their unique personalities and cultures rather than pretending to be someone they are not!

According to 13:5, "Love does not behave itself unseemly." Unseemly denotes unbecoming or indecent behavior. Love provokes one to treat his brethren in a decent manner. Rather than using racial jokes in conversations, Christians should try praising good leaders from other races. Respect for one another results in a set of Christ-centered standards. Our behavior should attest to the fact that we value one another.

Verse 5 also states that "Love seeketh not her own." Christians seeking to imitate Christ should be seeking the good of others (Philippians 2:1-5). Biblical love understands that it is more blessed to give than to receive. Racial reconciliation is better served by those who sincerely desire to empower others. God's desire is to use us to help our brethren.

Verse 5 further instructs that "Love is not easily provoked." This means that love is the negative of "to arouse to anger, to stir up." Love is more action than reaction. Saints should overcome evil with good rather than repaying evil with evil. There should be a greater concern for what one can do for his brother than what his brother has done, negatively, to him.

One's meditation has much influence upon his reactions. Feelings that our "rights" have been denied or that we have been treated unfairly naturally provoke us. Unresolved anger and bitterness cause some people to behave like emotional volcanoes, ready to erupt at the least provocation. To avoid such emotional bondage, one must cultivate a sweet moment by moment walk with the Savior. Trials, even racial injustices, must be viewed as opportunities for personal growth (Romans 5:3-5; James 1:2-5; 1 Peter 1:5-8).

The final characteristic of love mentioned in verse five is that "love thinketh no evil." The idea is that love does not take account of (that is, does not add up, does not reckon up) evil suffered to the point of considering the person who did the evil to be totally evil in character. Love does not dwell on past evil done to it. Such thinking tends to produce a perception of others – especially those who have hurt you – as totally evil. Such a perception has a tendency to interpret even good deeds as expressions of evil motives! Forgiveness allows one to develop beyond past mistakes. A lack of love freezes one into the past. Better relationships in the future will be built by those who learn to forgive.

The fact that love does not take account of evil does not mean that love rejoices in unrighteousness. Biblical love is not a good feeling about everyone or everything. In fact, verse 6 states explicitly that "love rejoiceth not in iniquity." Love does not rejoice when it sees a person in a condition of unrighteousness. This condition may refer to either the perpetrator or to the victim of injustice.

Love knows sin is destructive. Love, not only would not support, neither would it be satisfied with silence when fellow citizens, and sometimes fellow Christians, are being systematically humiliated, denied their legal rights, and killed in the land where life, liberty, and the pursuit of happiness are promised to all. Likewise, love finds no joy in the "convictions" of Christian leaders which drove them to deny black Christians the privilege of enrolling in their schools, serving with their agencies, or becoming members of their churches (Proverbs 14:34; Micah 2:1-4).

According to verse 6, a loving saint rejoices in the truth. When truth prevails in a life, love rejoices; for it knows that truth is good for the one loved. Christians must be committed to the proposition that obedience to the Word of God is good for all of mankind. We must lament over misinterpretations and misapplications of the Scripture to dehumanization and disenfranchisement of people, many of them Christians, based on their color. We must not rest until the Scriptural record is clear and our lives and institutions have been brought into conformity to the Bible. Anything less is destructive. Love seeks to build, not destroy. (See Proverbs 29:18; 3 John 4.)

Christian love is courageous – a courage that willfully, at personal cost, dares to protect, believe, hope, and persevere for the good of others. The race issue will be addressed best by people of such character who see and bring out redeemable aspects of people whom others have deserted.

Love, according to verse 7, "beareth all things." The word means to protect, or preserve, by covering, hence to hold something off which threatens, to bear up against, to hold out against, and so to endure, bear, forebear. The idea is to forego what is rightly due to one because to demand it would be destructive to the one responsible (1 Corinthians 9:12). What rights are we willing to surrender for the specific purpose of protecting a fellow believer? Black believers sometimes demand a greater understanding and empathy of the civil rights struggle than many of their white brethren possess. Rather than surrendering the right to be understood and seeking to educate their white brethren, some blacks simply withdraw.

Whites, on the other hand, expect a loyalty and pride from blacks to organizations which were built during a segregated, racist era. The heritage of many of these organizations – while having much to be proud of – is seriously deficient in racial and cultural understanding. Both sides need to identify issues which can simply be overlooked. All must remember that "love covers a multitudes of sin" (Proverbs 10:12).

Solid relationships are built upon mutual trust. One of the challenges of this litigious society is encouraging trust. When one turns to the courts, lawyers defend their clients with the attitude that there must be a loser and a winner. Often race relations debates are entered with a win-lose attitude as well. Yet, verse 7 says love "believeth all things." The idea is that love trusts, or has confidence, in the person. This does not demand blindly believing everything one says, but love upholds the other's character. Love will give one the benefit of the doubt until facts prove otherwise. Too often our cross-racial relationships are characterized by the opposite. There is a tendency to believe the worst until absolute proof of the contrary is demonstrated.

It has been said that the future is as bright as the promises of God. When it comes to race relations, we must look more to the promises of God than to history or to our present state. The present segregated nature of the majority of churches and the deep divide between saints of different colors can be discouraging for those who dare to believe that multiracial ministries are the will of God. Biblical love encourages confidence; for, according to verse 7, it "hopeth all things."

Although there are precious few models of successful multiracial ministries, love is confident that such ministries are the will of God and that they can be accomplished by His grace. Love believes that God will work in the hearts and minds of His people to produce the qualities necessary to enhance biblical multiracial fellowship. Love sees the confusion and struggle in seeking biblical relationships as periods of trial. During these times of trial, love – rather than giving up – believes that God is using these trials to perfect our character. Mature believers are needed to wrestle with issues that divide us and forge new paths to guide the Church along the road of racial healing (James 1:2-8).

Maintaining the status quo is less painful than making substantive change. Bringing substantive change in race relations within the Church will require blacks and whites who are willing to suffer. Rising above the injustices, stereotypes, and distrust which too often characterize our relationships will demand love which, according to verse 7, "endureth all things." "Endureth all things" denotes to abide under, to bear up courageously, especially under suffering. The word is used in 2 Timothy 2:10, 18 of Paul's suffering for the elects' sake and in Hebrews 12:2, 3 of Christ, enduring the cross for the joy set before him. All of this should encourage those who are committed to reconciliation that the supreme motivation, love, has the ability to endure in the face of unreturned love, and even in spite of suffering. *Love continues to obey even during the hard times.*

What the Church desperately needs now is love, God's love. It is a matter of obedience to Christ. Love is a badge of identification for true disciples. One dramatic illustration of a loving response to racial injustice is demonstrated by John Perkins, a black Christian, as reported in *He's My Brother: Former Racial Foes Offer Strategy for Reconciliation.* The book includes a vivid account of John's 1970 arrest and brutal beating by white policemen in Brandon, Mississippi. An all-white jury acquitted the policemen of all charges. Perkins' response to these injustices was a call for racial reconciliation. He and his family have lived out that message in Mississippi and in California. The following recounts the mental struggle and decision Dr. Perkins reached while recovering from the physical marks of racism after having been beaten all night by sheriff's deputies:

> *As I thought about things in the hospital, it took my mind back to Christ....*
>
> *Still I was tempted strongly to believe that ... America's white-controlled society would never be willing to share on an equal basis with those with black skin, or brown, or red, or yellow.... When you have been mistreated by a group of people ..., you think that (they) are representative of the entire race*
>
> *But ... God brought other white faces to my mind: white doctors who had tended to me in a caring, compassionate way; white attorneys who were standing beside me as I battled the state of Mississippi; white college graduates who were working for Voice of Calvary Ministries and earning only $100 a month; white preachers who had begun to speak out against racism and call for racial reconciliation. I thought of white kids like Doug Huemmer and*

*Ira Freshman, who had shared that night of terror in Bran-
don....*

*In Mississippi at that time, it seemed to me that these
were only a few positives against an overwhelming back-
drop of negatives.... Stronger than all these images ... was
another powerful ... scene ... the Son of God dying on the
cross ... bruised and battered, His back torn apart..., His
hands and feet pierced through with huge spikes and blood
running down His face from a crown of thorns.... ...He
cried out, "My God! My God! Why have You forsaken
Me?" Yet Christ ... prayed, "Father, forgive them, for they
know not what they do."*

*The Holy Spirit ... seemed to be whispering to me again
and again, "John, you've got to love them." ...*

*I might go so far as to say that I experienced a second
conversion while I lay in that hospital bed. ... a conversion
of love and forgiveness.* (Perkins, Tarrants, & Wimbish,
pages 131-133)

Chapter 10 – The Dilution of Truth

Popular proponents of secular multiculturalism, pluralism, and diversity – in an attempt to be all-inclusive – reveal themselves to be exclusive of those who hold to absolute truth. The battle is particularly fierce when it comes to moral truth. Moral stands are considered to be uninformed acts of hatred and bigotry. Such assumption is illustrated by an **anti**-antiabortion protest at Chicago's Armitage Baptist Church. Ignoring the church's peaceful, though persistent antiabortion activities, a protest was called to disrupt services at Armitage by a coalition involving such organizations as Queer Nation, Sister Serpents, and the National Committee to Free Puerto Rican POWs and Political Prisoners. A counter-rally was mounted by antiabortion forces, involving several South Side Chicago black churches. Thousands packed the Wednesday worship service. Men from the congregations blocked the entrance to the church. Choirs sang on the steps, drowning out chants from the anti-antiabortion forces. John Leo noted that:

The demonstrators seemed disorganized. With weeks of preparation and 10 sponsoring groups, only a hundred or so people turned out.

The most common chant was "Racist, sexist, antigay/Born-again bigots, go away." The racist charge is particularly weird: The Armitage congregation is roughly

30 percent black, 30 percent Hispanic and 40 percent white. (page 22)

Some evangelical/fundamental believers, likewise, see the surrender of truth in diversity issues such as racial reconciliation. Some major denominations are ordaining homosexuals. Others debate the reality of a literal hell and the accuracy or truthfulness of the Bible. Historically, these denominations have been more vocal in their support of civil rights than have religious conservatives. Therefore, some evangelical/-fundamentalists believe the racial reconciliation fervor to be an ecumenical agenda which will dilute the truth.

The Bible places a high premium on truth. Proverbs 23:23 encourages us to buy the truth and sell it not. God gave the Bible to communicate the way not only to salvation but to sanctification (how Christians should live) as well. (See Psalm 1; 1 Corinthians 3:10-15; 2 Timothy 3:16-4:4; 1 Peter 1:22 – 2:2.) Before bringing the light of truth upon the dark subject of diversity, it may be beneficial to examine some of the myths by which we live.

The Myths by Which We Live

Frequently whites will ask why are people using hyphens, for example, African-Americans, Asian-Americans, Arab-Americans and Native-Americans? What's wrong with just being Americans, they question? There seems to be a belief that we were all equal citizens until some ungrateful unpatriotic people began to divide the country. The fact is that some Americans were classified and treated as less than citizens by white Americans. The Dred Scott decision is a historical testimony to this fact. This Supreme Court pronouncement held that blacks were not protected by the U.S. Constitution.

The entire race designation or choice is built upon lies. One wonders why a person whose ancestry includes European and African blood is designated black or African American. According to the 1990 census the majority of black Americans are of mixed ancestry. Obviously, neither the designation nor the choice to identify oneself as African American is based upon fact. This classification system derives from a white obsession with a pure gene pool.

The power structure occasionally had to make judgments when genetic ancestry alone was not sufficient to designate one's race. Plessy versus Ferguson was such an instance which resolved the question for a century or so.

Plessy, a southern businessman, was 7/8 white, which meant that race mixing occurred among his great-grandparents. One of his eight great-grandparents was of African descent. Plessy filed a suit against a railroad for being denied his accustomed access to the white sections of the train. The Supreme Court ruled in 1856 that anyone with a drop of "black" blood was black. The resulting reverberations caused many of mixed blood and mixed marriages to flee the South.

Opposition to such arbitrary classification is growing. Public voice demanded that the census provide a category for persons to classify themselves as *other* (race) in addition to the traditional choices. Another group desires the ability to acknowledge the multiplicity of their family tree. Perhaps it is time for us as a church, if not a nation, to consider Russia's abolishment of classifications based upon race.

The Soviet Union used a complex system dating back to the czars. Formerly an empire that included many conquered countries with many ethnic groups who have been bitter enemies from time immemorial, the USSR stretched across vast areas of Asia and Europe and recognized 103 separate ethnic groups. Identification papers carried one's ethnic designation right under one's name. Discrimination, affirmative action, and brutality were practiced freely – generally with racist or political motives – aided by the state-run system of ethnic labeling. At age 16, mixed children were forced to choose to be known by one parent's ethnicity. In the face of all of this, the new Russian government has chosen to eliminate racial accounting.

White Superiority

In the States, the ruling class of European descent crafted an historical account which overlooked, co-opted, or deleted the contributions of blacks and other minorities. There was a clear portrayal of white superiority. This distortion of history seems to have had as its foundation the evolutionary myth of the survival of the fittest. Such thinking, a desire for superiority, seems to motivate many black Americans' fascination with their roots. The power and rule of blacks of past generations, especially Africa, is promoted, often to demonstrate the superiority of blacks over whites.

While integrity demands that one acknowledge white historians' denial of contributions of blacks to history, it likewise demands the whole truth. The whole truth is that while blacks made great contributions to society, they had their fair share of sinners as well. Many of us have grown accustomed to seeing the Pharaohs who enslaved Israel as oppressors and as enemies of God. We have embraced the cry "let my people go" as the cry of the righteous for deliverance from the unrighteous. But we sometimes refuse to accept the logical conclusion when the Egyptians Pharaohs are said to have been black. Our history, as well as the history of whites, is blighted with sin. From black Africans' participation in the slave trade to mass destruction of human life in Uganda and Rwanda, it is evident that sin is no respecter of persons. In fact, if one would follow the root system to its beginning, one would find Adam. All of mankind germinated from the seed of Adam. Consequently, all of mankind has been infected with the deadly disease of sin. (See Romans 5:12.)

There is a myth of racial unity. When criticizing each other, we like to talk in terms of what all blacks or all whites believe or do. Such language perpetuates a myth. The word *all* needs to be reserved for very few occasions. We know that *all* have sinned (Romans 3:23). Often when speaking in a church whose membership is predominantly white, I have been asked, "Does Jesse Jackson speak for all blacks?"

I answer with the question, "Does Bill Clinton speak for all whites?" After a moment of laughter, everyone seems to get the point. There are different beliefs, values, and leaders within racial groups.

The media has created the myth that crime is primarily perpetrated by blacks. While crime in black communities is a grave concern, it was not black people who orchestrated the Savings and Loan scandal. Human cannibal Jeffery Drummer, mad man Charles Manson, and Dr. Death (Jack Kevorkian) are but a few fair-skinned menaces to society. Yet some whites (and some blacks, as well) have an immediate sense of danger in the presence of blacks while feeling secure in the presence of whites.

Likewise blacks, especially black males, will speak of the humiliation of being followed by a white security guard in a suburban mall. Sometimes the response is that one will never shop in the store again. The same young black male speaks of returning to "the hood" with his "homeys" (home boys, or fellow blacks), where he is "safe." The reality is that a black male's chance of being killed by a department store security guard today is rare. However the leading cause of death for young black males is homicide by a homey.

Another myth is that to be truly black one must be an inner city, ebonics speaking, low income, criminally disposed, and uneducated individual. Blacks with good jobs and who live in middle to upper middle class neighborhoods are considered "sell-outs." They are said to have forgotten who they are and are trying to be white. Several parents have told me that their high school children who were performing very well academically, were told by other black students that academic excellence was a "white thing!" Such erroneous perceptions and statements cry out for a proper perspective of history – not to prove superiority – but to document the excellence of contribution of black Americans who rose above and shattered obstacles the like of which this generation has not faced.

Racism is a reality, but so is mythological thinking. Christians need to be committed to speaking the truth in love with a view toward growing in our knowledge of Christ and working together for mutual benefit (Ephesians 4:15-16). Let us reject the myths and receive the truth. Truth is to be discovered from a literal, grammatical, historical interpretation of the Holy Scriptures.

Truth Matters

After I addressed medical students at a secular campus on the subject of racial reconciliation, the meeting was opened for questions. One student introduced himself and stated that he was a Muslim. He explained that he believed in a different way to heaven than I had articulated during my presentation. Then he asked, in light of our different beliefs about how one is saved, did I ever speak about religious reconciliation?

I responded to his question with an illustration. I asked him to imagine that a dying patient was lying between the two of us. According to his training, the patient's life could only be saved by performance of a very precise surgical procedure. I asked, what would his response be if I came and said that I wanted to perform a surgery contrary to what the best of medical science promises will save this patient's life. I reasoned, I am sure out of love for the patient and professional integrity you would oppose my performing a surgery which would be fatal. My application of the illustration was that due to my love of people and belief that Jesus Christ is the way, the truth, and the life and no man comes to the Father but through Him (see

John 14:6), I could not seek religious peace at the price of letting him go into an eternal hell. Love for you and your eternal destiny compels me to tell you the truth, I said in conclusion. Even Christians are downplaying truth. They declare that doctrine divides. The denominational walls that divide us must be broken down, they insist. It is much easier to destroy than it is to build. Some Christians are guilty of believing and/or implying that only members of their church or denomination are saved. Others demand complete conformity to every teaching and practice of their church for a saint to be considered in fellowship with God. Such erroneous thinking must not serve as an excuse for saints to stop diligently seeking a proper understanding of Scripture to discern how a Christian should live. (See 2 Timothy 2:14-19.) The apostle Paul commended the saints at Berea for testing his words by Scripture. (See Acts 17:11.)

Truth really does matter. Consider the fact that Paul said if he or an angel from heaven preached a different gospel than what was already preached, the messenger of the new gospel was to be accursed (Galatians 1:8-9). We are told not to welcome those who deny that Jesus Christ is come in the flesh. (See 2 John 1:7-11) The saints were warned against being contaminated through philosophy and vain deceit after the tradition of men and not after Christ (Colossians 2:9). Timothy was left in Ephesus to assure that correct doctrine was taught (1 Timothy 1:3-11). Some were turned over to Satan because of denying the faith (1 Timothy 1:19-20). Others clearly rejected doctrine and were noted for doing so (1 Timothy 6:20-21; 2 Timothy 2:17-18; Titus 1:10-17; 3:10-11).

Indeed sound doctrine or teaching should characterize any minister of the Gospel. The Bible is our textbook for ministry (2 Timothy 3:16-17). Those who have the gift of speaking in the church are to speak as the oracles of God (1 Peter 4:10-11). One is to rightly divide, or seek clear understanding, of the in-

tent of a given passage, the Word of truth (2 Timothy 2:15).
Many of the New Testament books were written for the express
purpose of giving doctrinal clarity to saints who were being
swayed by error, including 1 Corinthians, Galatians, Colossians, 2 Thessalonians, 1 Timothy, Titus, Hebrews, and 1 John.
Furthermore, the New Testament warns against false prophets
who will be teaching erroneous doctrine which must be refuted.
(See 2 Corinthians 11:1-23; Galatians 2:7; 3:1; Philippians 3:1-
2; 1 Timothy 4:1-3; 2 Timothy 3:1-9; 4:3; 2 Peter 2:1-3; Jude
3-4.) The Church dares not, in the name of racial reconciliation
or any other issue, deny the importance that God places upon
sound doctrine. (See Proverbs 29:18; Hosea 4:6.)

The truth of the matter is that some things do not matter. A
black pastor took several associate members from his church to
the historic Moody Pastors' conference in Chicago. Moody is
known for having the prince of preachers minister to the hearts
of pastors. Toward the end of the conference, the black pastor
asked the associate how he was enjoying the conference. The
associate responded by asking when would they hear some
good preaching! Good preaching to him was more style than
substance.

I know of several instances where white Bible college or
seminary professors felt constrained to warn students that a
black church was not sound in the faith because the membership said *amen* while the preacher was delivering his sermon or
the choir clapped and swayed while singing. These cases involved doctrinally sound pastors, who in some cases were
graduates from the institutions which criticized their style.

Must all mature Christians dress alike, share identical mu-
sical taste, belong to one political party and agree on one style
of worship? Does the Scripture address this issue? Scripture
has not left the church to preference on these matters, but has
given us the principles of conscience and love instead. Christian liberty is a biblical doctrine. The major passages teaching

on the subject are Acts 15; 1 Corinthians 8-11; Romans 14-15; and Colossians 3:10-15. These passages clearly argue for diversity with unity rather than uniformity. Christian liberty and conscience are precious biblical truths. The emphasis is upon love, personal sacrifice, acceptance of others, and a nonjudgmental attitude with a view toward maintaining unity and assisting spiritual growth.

The church would be well served by establishing a biblical list of doctrinal and moral positions which must not be surrendered and a list of disputable matters concerning which saints may disagree without being charged with disobedience to God (Romans 14:1-12). All must be warned that while personal conscience is critical in making liberty choices, God never leads one to use the principle of Christian liberty to serve the flesh (Galatians 6:13). (Flesh in this context is not the physical body but refers to inner sinful desires which crave activities contrary to the Word of God and biblical morality.)

Truth Teaches One Humanity and One Body

Segregated churches and ministries seem to be the norm in America. Is such color coordination conformity to truth or the fruit of misinterpretation of Scripture? Segregated churches, just as the segregated American society, are the fruit seeds of prejudice, disguised as truth, planted and nurtured for generations in various forms. Today we are still reaping the harvest of a misdirected church due to misinterpretation and misapplication of Scripture with regard to race relations within the church.

Recently after I had preached on the subject of racial reconciliation at a white church, the pastor came forward and addressed the congregation. He felt constrained to share a personal story about his father. His father had been a strong conservative and had served on the 1976 George Wallace campaign. As an insurance salesman, he estimated that his father had been in over thirty thousand homes throughout his career. Only once could his father ever remember being asked by the owner to leave a home. The pastor related the story as he recalled his father's sharing with the family in tears after being put out of the house.

The pastor's father, who had recently received Christ, looked forward to visiting a deacon's home to explain his insurance program and to fellowship around spiritual matters. During a time of fellowship the deacon mentioned, "I'm proud to be American, Christian, and white." The father responded that he understood the American and Christian parts, but did not understand why the deacon added white to the list of things for which he was proud? The deacon responded that he wasn't one of those n-word lovers.

The pastor's father exclaimed, "I cannot believe you said that. My Bible teaches that God loves all of us, red, yellow, black and white." At this point the deacon's wife exclaimed, "I have already prayed that before my daughter marry an n-word that God would kill her." At this point the salesman was asked to leave the home.

Preservation of the purity and superiority of the white race has been a guiding American principle for decades. Laws against interracial marriage were only overruled by the supreme court in 1967 in Loving versus Virginia. A 1997 "Dateline NBC" special with Tom Brokaw ("Why can't we live together?") identified the fear of interracial marriage as a major motivation for segregated communities.

The sad fact is that the Church has a greater conformity to the world than to the Word in this matter of segregation. The church has been guilty of placing a tradition of men on the level of divine truth. Many evangelical/fundamental institutions were founded and fostered by leadership which supported a segregated church. Denial to blacks of access to church sanctuaries, baptismal pools, membership, Christian schools, and Bible colleges was a symbol of uncompromising convictions based upon biblical teaching.

In the 1970s and 1980s, Bob Jones University became a symbol for many as BJU fought all the way to the federal appellate court for their right not to accept blacks into their university. After losing the antidiscrimination case, Bob Jones University simply refused government aid for the freedom to deny admission to saints who had a passion for taking the Word of God around the world. At the heart of Bob Jones' concern about a diverse racial student body was the desire to prohibit the "sin" of interracial marriage. Various Bible passages were appealed to for divine sanction on such practices.

Interracial marriage, especially between blacks and whites, is one area where man's interpretation of the Bible must be cleansed from cultural bias. Christians are called to obey the Bible. Truth must take precedence over tradition. (See Mark 7:5-14.) Divine sanction rests only upon the Word of God as it is rightly divided, or properly interpreted. "Conviction" based upon an erroneous interpretation of a text is false doctrine. False doctrine must be confronted and corrected.

Over the years, I have heard many texts which are supposed to demonstrate God's disapproval of interracial marriage. We will look at a few of the more logical ones and seek to put forth an accurate interpretation of the texts. The texts will be underlined below. My comments will follow the underlined text.

One text which has served as a foundation for everything from the dehumanizing of black people to racial segregation is Genesis 9 and 10. It is argued that Genesis 9:18-25 teaches that Ham, which means *black* according to proponents of this argument, thereby denoting him as the father of all blacks, was cursed and committed to a life of servitude throughout all succeeding generations. Based upon this interpretation, blacks have been enslaved, discriminated against, and segregated in

society. To intermarry with a black would pollute the superior
race. The whole argument is based on a shaky premise. Scholars say that Ham actually means *hot*.

The *New International Study Bible* has the following note
on Genesis 9:25:

> *Cursed be Canaan! Some maintain that Ham's son (see*
> *vv. 18, 22) was to be punished because of their father's sin*
> *(see Exodus 20:5), but Exodus 20 restricts such punishment*
> *to "those who hate me." It is probably better to hold that*
> *Canaan and his descendants were to be punished because*
> *they were going to be even worse than Ham (Leviticus*
> *18:2-3, 6-10). Lowest of slaves, Joshua's subjection of the*
> *Gibeonites (Joshua 9:27) is one of the fulfillments (see also*
> *Joshua 16:10; Judges 1:28, 30, 33, 35; 1 Kings 9:20-21).*
> *Noah's prophecy cannot be used to justify the enslavement*
> *of blacks, since those cursed here were Canaanites, who*
> *were Caucasian.*

Some argue that the dividing of people by languages at the
Tower of Babel demonstrates God's desire to keep the races
separated (Genesis 11). The logical conclusion is that since
God separated the races the church should seek to maintain
what God has created. Thus interracial marriage is contrary to
the will of God.

Application of any text must be preceded by correct interpretation. Several factors are critical for a proper interpretation
of this text. First, it should be noted that the people were all
one. This unity, in itself, is nowhere in the text said to be
wrong. According to the text, God was disturbed by the people's intention to build a tower to heaven. It was the act of
building the tower which caused God to confuse their languages, thereby weakening them and causing their building
project to fail. The text speaks of God's disapproval of men
uniting to accomplish goals contrary to His will. This has no

prohibition against two Christians seeking to do the will of God, which may include interracial marriage.

If the text were addressing segregation and/or intermarriage, the application should address language groups not races or colors. Thus different language *groups* within the same race would be prohibited from marriage! Language groups differ within races and transcend some races. Applying the text as divine teaching against interracial marriage is simply a cultural bias.

Acts 17:26, where it is stated that God "determined ... the bounds of their habitation," has been interpreted to mean that God has established the nations and does not approve of interracial marriage. The concept is that God established national or racial boundaries and man sins when he crosses these boundaries. While the text speaks of national, not racial boundaries, its emphasis is upon the unity rather than differences between men. The emphasis is upon all men's unity, *from one blood.* All have sinned and must repent, regardless of their nationality. It must be kept in mind, too, that the national boundaries which the text states God has established, do not harmonize well with man's race division by color. Many nations have people of different races or colors. Furthermore, if the text is teaching that people are not to marry across national boundaries, the application should prohibit intermarriage between Italians and Germans, French and Norwegian, and so forth. The issue should be national not racial.

Appeals to Old Testament Scriptures forbidding marriage with other races (Leviticus 21:14; Deuteronomy 7:3; 20:16-18; 1 Kings 11:1, 8; Ezra 10:2, 11, 14, 17, 18, 44; Nehemiah 13:23, 26) have been made to demonstrate God's displeasure with interracial marriage between Christians. God's concern about Israel's intermarriage with members of other nations was religious rather than racial. Intermarriage could, and did, result in the Israelites' being drawn into idolatry and an adulterous worship.

God gave principles to govern intermarriage with other nations (Deuteronomy 21:10-14). There are several notable marriages between Israelites and members of foreign nations, such as Rahab and Ruth (Matthew 1:5). A proper application of the prohibition of the Old Testament Scriptures would be the New Testament prohibition of marriage between saved and unsaved individuals (1 Corinthians 6:14-18).

Numbers 36:6, according to some, indicates that people with closer backgrounds have better marriages. Their application is that racial difference necessarily translates into cultural differences, assuring the failure of interracial marriages.

First, the assumption that racial differences naturally mean different cultural backgrounds is not true. Two individual of the same race but raised in different environments (for example, rural versus inner city) may have greater cultural differences than two of different races raised in similar environments. Furthermore, as far as Numbers 36:6 is concerned, the text is addressing a legal inheritance question not a racial issue (Numbers 36:9; 27:1-11). Notice that the issue involves there being no male to claim the land distributed to the family. The objective is to keep the land within the family. Therefore, a near relative is needed.

Another argument against interracial marriage has been the appeal to Scriptures forbidding marriage to "strange women." "Strange women" in the Scriptures refers to "foreign" or "of another race" (Proverbs 2:16; 5:3, 20; 6:24; 7:5; 20:16; 23:27; 27:13; Malachi 2:11). Examination of these texts demonstrates the concern was one of morality rather than interracial marriage. These texts are addressing prostitution and adultery, not interracial marriage (Proverbs 2:16, 17; 6:24; 23:27).

When all else fails the catch-all principle is expediency (Galatians 6:13; Romans 13:10; 2 Corinthians 6:12; 9:5, 6; 8:13; 9:19; 10:32). It is stated that while the Scriptures may not directly prohibit interracial marriage and while it may be lawful, it is certainly not wise. A mature believer would never enter into such a union.

Examples of intermarriage include: Joseph and Asenath (Genesis 41:45, 50-52); Moses and Zipporah (Numbers 12:1-2; Exodus 2:15-27); Rahab (Matthew 1:5); Ruth and Chilion (Ruth 1:2-5); Ruth and Boaz (Ruth 4:10; Matthew 1:15).

The expediency principle is applied to issues where the individual has the freedom to do or refrain from an action. As long as one does not commit sin, the issue becomes one of wisdom. Wisdom in one situation is not the same in another. There may well be situations where interracial marriage is unwise. Likewise, there may be situations where it is wise. We must be careful in judging those whose decision may be contrary to what we would prefer. The issue is who are we to determine the will of God for another in such a critical decision as marriage.

Conclusion

February of 1998 will be a memorable time in my life for two reasons. First, I accepted to speak for three days at the Northwest Baptist Seminary in Tacoma, Washington. Mark Wagner, president, had asked me to speak at a local church, also. Upon my agreement, I was scheduled to speak at the Antioch Bible Church. I had no previous knowledge of this church.

I arrived in Tacoma late Saturday night. On Sunday morning I spoke at three morning services to around 1500 people – people of various colors, nationalities and racial/cultural backgrounds. I spoke from John 13:34-35 on the subject of "color me love." The reception was wonderful. Senior Pastor Ken

Hutcherson and I experienced an immediate bonding. His wife, Nancy, invited several others and myself to their house for an afternoon of fun and fellowship. What a wonderful modern day model Antioch Bible Church is of the New Testament multiracial church located at Antioch in Acts 13. There was such a harmony between Antioch's vision and that of Baptist Bible College of Indianapolis that I believe a lifetime friendship has been born.

The second experience began with a phone call on Thursday afternoon February 26. My executive vice president called to inform me that my son had been injured at basketball practice and was being transported to the hospital. I immediately called the hospital. After identifying myself as the father the nurse told me that my son had suffered a 4-vertebrate fracture and was paralyzed from the shoulders down. She asked if I would like to speak to my wife who was coming down the hall at that moment. My wife said, "Matt is injured and it doesn't look good. I have to go now. The ambulance is about to transfer him to a different hospital."

This event opened a new chapter in our family's life. From the time of the phone call until this day, God has used Matt's injury to, among other things, create a multiracial event. Prayers chains were activated like a virus throughout the body of Christ. We received statements of prayer support from numerous states and over 32 foreign countries. Thousands of Christians from various races, cultures, and nations were united as they approached the throne of our Father on behalf of my family. We are appreciative of every member of the family of God who reached up to God and out to us during our time of need. I am thankful that I am a part of the family of God.

I will be eternally grateful for whites too innumerable to give individual mention who have ministered grace to me. These include my wife, the two men who led me to Christ, my pastor Kimber Kauffman (who clearly and boldly proclaims and practices racial reconciliation from the pulpit and in private), Christian leaders, co-workers, and friends. Together we must model a better message than what we inherited concerning race relations.

In this book I have sought to share some of my motivation and theology for being committed to biblical racial reconciliation. It is my conviction that racial reconciliation is the brainchild of God. It is rooted in redemption and should be guided by divine revelation. Christian obedience requires that we endeavor to maintain the unity of the Spirit in the bond of peace. My desire is that when I stand before the judgment seat of Christ He might say, "Your testimony to the world was clear because you loved your God and your neighbor. The Gospel message was more convincing in your generation because of your love for the people of God." Oh, may this indeed be the generation of reconciliation.

Appendix

(I am indebted to William Banks (*The Black Church*) for
the inspiration to add this survey.)

A Survey of African American History

Roots: 1619-1776 – Early Slave Trade

It seems that the Portuguese and the Spanish were the first Europeans to deal in the black slave trade. With the approval of the necessary governments in Africa, Europe, North America, and the Caribbean, and the tacit support of the Roman Catholic Church, slave traders maintained that "christianized" slaves were better off than free heathen.

Contrary to popular knowledge, not all blacks who reached the shores of North America were slaves. Thirty blacks were with Balboa when he discovered the Pacific Ocean in 1513. Estevanico accompanied Cabeza de Vaca from Florida into Mexico between 1528 and 1534.

Later the English, Dutch, and French entered the slave-trading picture, establishing stations in West Africa. By 1786, American and English ships carried the bulk of the trade. Africans, as well as whites, were involved in capturing and selling nearly twenty million Africans over the span of some 300 years (1517-1840).

The Middle Passage

The trip from the Gulf of Guinea to the New World was called the Middle Passage. It is estimated that twelve million Africans landed in Latin America and about two million were brought to the U.S. The other six million died en route. Some died resisting capture. Some died in captivity while being held in Africa waiting to be shipped out. Many committed suicide. Some, beaten and too weak to continue the trek in the coffle (similar to a chain gang), were abandoned to die.

The first black slaves to arrive in the U.S. were twenty who landed at Jamestown, VA, on August 20, 1619, from a Dutch frigate. Actually, they were indentured servants. There was little comparison of African slaves with European immigrants. For the slaves, all memories of Africa were extinguished. Family ties were destroyed. Members of the same tribe were separated as a safeguard against revolt. Families were split up for economic reasons.

Revival: 1777-1819

The Protestant Episcopal Church developed a reactionary approach. Its adherents were tired of seeing slaves belittled. Fears that conversion meant freedom from slavery were allayed. These U.S.-based Anglicans were the first Protestant missionaries to evangelize blacks. As noble as the intent was, the necessity of knowing the Anglican creed, catechism, and ritual made it difficult for the uneducated black masses to accept Christ in the Protestant Episcopal Church.

Sensing the need for an indigenized, contextualized Christian expression where blacks would feel welcome, St. Thomas Church was organized by Absalom Jones. Without relationships to a denomination or a mission organization, this black church was dedicated in 1794 in Philadelphia, PA. They immediately applied for membership in the Pennsylvania Diocese, but were not accepted until 1865. The church still exists. Its original charter limited membership to black people.

Work of Various Denominations

In addition, there was the Great Awakening of 1720 and later years. As a result of the revival, missionary zeal grew. Baptists and Methodists attracted many slaves, probably because of their simplicity of service and lack of ritual.

Quakers were at the forefront of the battle against slavery, but very few blacks were attracted to them.

The Rise of the Negro Preacher

As the so-called black churches began to increase in numbers and to affiliate with denominational bodies, whites supplied preachers for Negro churches. Further, as might be expected, white ministers preached in white churches where Negroes were allowed to attend. Occasionally Negro exhorters were allowed to speak from the floor, but not from the pulpit.

In spite of that, some free Negro preachers became well known. For instance, Lemuel Haynes – who was born in Connecticut in 1753 and served in the Revolutionary War – was one of the first Negroes in America to pastor a white congregation. Samuel Ringgold Ward pastored a white congregation in Cortlandville, NY. Preaching was an outlet for leadership ability, and it was an office of prestige. Therefore, preaching became an office to be coveted.

Blacks were able to worship in three distinct types of churches which existed during the slavery era.

- White churches with blacks as members of the congregation.
- Separate black churches under white leadership and supervision. Examples of this latter type include: Silver

Bluff, North Carolina, 1773-1775; and Negro Baptist Church in Georgia, January 20, 1788.
* Separate black churches with black leadership. The most prominent example of this type was Bethel African Methodist Episcopal Church, organized by Richard Allen in 1794.

In addition, Baptists established black congregations in Maryland, Virginia, Georgia, Kentucky, and other locations.

Reaction: 1820-1865

In retrospect, perhaps abolitionists should have anticipated a backlash. For all its evils, slavery was a very lucrative segment of the southern economy. One important contributor was the recently invented cotton gin and the consequent increased value of the slave. When the choice was between human rights and money, money won out. The economic component was so overriding that – although Congress had passed a law in 1807 forbidding the African slave trade – smuggling continued, and laws against interstate kidnapping were violated. In short, in the South, economics and racism won out over abolition.

Another factor leading to emancipation had to do with the unpredictable slave revolts which stirred fear in the hearts of many southern whites. In 1822, Denmark Vesey, a free Negro carpenter in Charleston, SC, planned an extensive revolt but was betrayed. He and 35 others were hanged. In 1831 Nat Turner led a bloody insurrection at Southhampton County, VA, killing some 55 whites before he and 16 of his followers were captured and hanged.

The revolts were attributed to Negro preachers' being brainwashed by white abolitionists. Consequently, restrictions were imposed. In 1823, Mississippi made it unlawful for six or more Negroes to meet for educational purposes. Religious meetings required the master's permission and white supervision. In 1831 in Delaware, no more than 12 blacks were allowed to assemble later than midnight unless there were three respectable whites present. Because the Church was instrumental in the education of slaves, these restrictions served to arrest educational advancement and to compound ignorance. By 1845 only 15 Negro Sabbath schools existed in the south, with 1,489 pupils attending.

New Testament Scripture and Slavery

While saluting the proverbial "Give me liberty or give me death," Southern slavemasters at the same time selectively read and interpreted the Bible to affirm slavery as they practiced it. 1 Timothy 6:1 was a favorite passages:

> *All who are under the yoke of slavery should consider their masters worthy of full respect, so that God's name and our teaching may not be slandered.* (NIV)

Perhaps a large number of citizens of the New World did not know that New Testament slavery was not barbaric in nature, such as that practiced in the South.

It would seem that true ministers of the Gospel would have risen up in droves to call attention of the verse which reads: "Love your neighbor as yourself" (Matthew 22:39; Luke 10:27). After having said that the greatest commandment is to love God, Jesus Himself equates love of neighbor to love of God. Well might the slavemasters, "desiring to justify (themselves)," have asked, "Who is my neighbor?" What more appropriate response than the parable which Jesus told about the Good Samaritan who, at some inconvenience to himself, aided a mugging victim? Jesus' selection of main characters was deliberate in that the mugged man was of a race/culture who considered themselves "superior" to the race/culture of the man who provided the much-needed assistance. On a good day, the Jew would have no dealing with the Samaritan. However, the mugged man was in no position to stand on ceremony when the Samaritan extended help to the helpless Jew.

If slavemasters had only been willing to take a look at the book of Philemon, they would have had difficulty justifying the practice of slavery. Addressed to the Christian slavemaster Philemon, the letter makes it clear that Paul is not in favor of slavery: "I could be bold and order you to do what you ought to do, yet I appeal to you on the basis of love" (Philemon 8-9).

What might Paul order Philemon to do? Simple. The first thing involved forgiving the theft which Onesimus had committed prior to running away to get lost in the big city – Rome. (Onesimus' getting involved with Paul indicates that you can't hide from God – even in the big city where no one knows you.)

The second thing is, as Paul says, "yet I appeal to you on the basis of love." Paul goes on to say:

Perhaps the reason he was separated from you for a little while was that you might have him back for good – no longer a slave, but better than a slave, as a dear brother. (Philemon 15-16, NIV)

Slavery, as practiced in the Old Testament, had escape clauses. First, a slave could purchase his or her freedom. Secondly, a kinsman-redeemer could purchase a slave's freedom. Thirdly, the Year of Jubilee meant freedom for all slaves with the exception of those who chose to remain in bondage. An escaped slave would be returned to his master when captured. But the Year of Jubilee was an event to be waited for with more eagerness than "they that watch for the morning."

Events Leading Up to the Civil War

I will always value books as important conveyers of values. Some spokesmen are grateful that Harriet Beecher Stowe's 1852 *Uncle Tom's Cabin* was a major force in enlightening them to the atrocities of slavery. In isolation, this may have been just another book. However, its impact was multiplied, combined as it was with the increasing polarization between pro- and anti-slavery forces, related legal decisions (such as the

Dred Scott decision, 1857), and revolts (such as the John Brown rebellion, 1859). These forces drove the country toward its bloodiest war on American soil. Leadership fell to Abraham Lincoln, who was elected to the presidency in 1860 for just such a time as this.

Reconstruction and Retaliation: 1866-1914

Following the Civil War, many in the South were reluctant to relinquish control over their former subjects. The terms of surrender required that the South honor the Emancipation Proclamation. Affirmative action was pursued aggressively to provide the new Americans with full participation in the affairs of this country. Congressmen were elected from their ranks. Things started to improve in many other vital areas.

There was widespread refusal, however, to welcome the newly freed slaves to the society of free men and women. Union soldiers enforced freedom for blacks until national behind-the-scenes politics resulted in the withdrawal of Union forces, leaving a largely unlettered, unsophisticated people to fend for themselves in very hostile territory. With no significant power, blacks were at the mercy of southern politicians, police, businesspeople, and spiteful people-on-the-streets.

Jim Crow "is a slang term for the post-Civil War practices of systematically segregating and suppressing the American black man" (Banks, page 33), many of which practices were codified into law. Whether written into law or not, the Ku Klux Klan mentality permitted whites to have their way with blacks in ways that are almost too brutal and unthinkable even for late night TV.

Blacks were denied access to public places, a practice that lasted throughout their first century of freedom. I remember the appearance in the 1960s of an activist group with the Swahili name *Uhuru* (Freedom Now!). In the 1950s, Jackie Robinson was not permitted to eat in white-only restaurants as he traveled with the Brooklyn Dodgers in the South. The Civil Rights movement of the 1960s, under the leadership of Rev. Dr. Martin Luther King, Jr., encountered untold inhuman atrocities as non-violent blacks and their white supporters marched, sat in, and otherwise exposed the citadels of white supremacy in American society. Men, women, and children were rebuffed by fire hoses, electric cattle prods, axe handles, police brutality, lynchings, drownings, bombings, and more atrocities too numerous to mention here. There were separate water fountains, one marked "white only," one marked "colored" (as blacks were known earlier in this century, a term they consider an insensitive insult today).

Blacks who traveled through the South found it necessary to go self-contained because of the unavailability of accommodations for their families. This gave rise to the very common picnic basket of fried chicken and related trimmings, as well as the portable potty for the little ones whose bladders were not able to hold on for the long stretches between safe, friendly facilities.

Nor have all these attitudes been entirely eradicated from the self-concepts of some whites in the South (or in the North, for that matter). Even in the seventies, former Detroit Mayor Coleman Young scored major points with his black constituents when he disbanded the notorious STRESS police units which reportedly administered police brutality with a vengeance. Fortunately, there are large numbers of whites and blacks in politics, business, and other endeavors who promote equality. Some even promote brotherhood. Some advocate compensatory inequality (in favor of the formerly oppressed) to have America attempt to make up for its history of systematic oppression. Opponents are winning the day, ironically, by attacking affirmative action as a white civil rights issue.

The Reconstruction Period: 1866-1914

Because of the personal convictions of President Abraham Lincoln, the Emancipation Proclamation was passed in 1863 and brought freedom to the slaves – but not equality. In fact, the news of the Emancipation Proclamation was withheld from Texas slaves until June of that year. In some circles, that late revelation is celebrated under the name Juneteenth.

In the early 1870s, following the Civil War, seven Negroes were elected to Congress at the same time. Twenty were elected to the House of Representatives during that decade. Progress was short-lived, however. As noted above, the withdrawal of Federal troops from the South marked the beginning of the end of equal rights.

The Ku Klux Klan (KKK) was formed to defend the white race from a so-called international Jewish-communist conspiracy. The civil rights movement was later considered to be a front for the conspiracy. Consequently, the KKK made it their purpose to reduce the effectiveness of the civil rights movement by any means possible. They made it their objective to abuse black civil rights leaders, Jewish leaders, individuals who spoke up for civil rights, and often randomly chosen, relatively helpless individuals. The KKK is fairly well known for its white costume and mask with a pointed hood. Their trademark tactics included the burning of crosses on the lawns of their victims, lynchings, and bombings – usually by large numbers of Klan members. The intent was to discourage blacks and Jews from full participation in the political, social, and economic processes by creating an atmosphere of terror that made the price too high for most people to risk.

One result was that blacks were weeded out of office. At the same time, new laws were established to enforce racial segregation and to keep blacks "in their place," a popular Jim Crow expression.

Voting qualifications were set up which blacks could not meet. Tests were given as a screening instrument to see if blacks were intelligent enough to vote. Another hurdle was the "grandfather" test, which limited registration to applicants whose grandfathers had voted. This clearly eliminated the descendants of former slaves. The combination of these tactics took their toll. Whereas in 1896 there were 130,334 Negroes registered to vote, in 1904, only 1,342 were registered voters.

The assault against the black race came from all levels. In 1896, even the Supreme Court added momentous blows to the fray by creating the infamous "separate but equal" facilities decree. In spite of all this opposition, this period witnessed tremendous church growth in the black community. One reason was the fact that the Church spoke effectively to the frustrating secular conditions faced by blacks: In many cases, their family lives were severely strained by violence, bigoted job practices, and more. Black families were penalized by a distorted view of the proper male image which had become a part of the world-view of slaves after two centuries of slavery. Unfortunately descendants of slaves encountered a lot of difficulty in shaking this negative self-concept of the role of the male in the family.

In the meantime, crime flourished in the black community as if the system wanted to see decent, but helpless, people victimized by a lawless element of their own people. The authorities did little to counteract the crime wave which spread like a cancer through institutions of value to the black community. In addition, blacks did not receive adequate financial and administrative support for their separate but equal schools.

Furthermore, many blacks lived with the reality that their civil rights, if not also their very lives, could be abused at any time. It made little sense to report a racial incident. There would likely be no arrest or conviction relating to hate crimes.

Movements in the African American Community Today

The history of mankind on this globe is one movement after another. In modern times, the black community has its share of movements, some of which have become institutionalized and almost have a life of their own. These include black theology, Afrocentrism, the Black Muslims (Nation of Islam), and the Black Church.

Black theology officially is an outgrowth of the Black Power movement of the sixties. It emerged from the need of black people to think theologically for themselves. According to Cone and Wilmore:

> The pioneers of early Black theology were determined to extrapolate from the concept of Black Power a theological referent that would not only vindicate the young civil rights workers laboring in the rural South, who wanted to apply more severe sanctions against white die-hards, but would also galvanize the left wing of the Southern-based civil rights movement and reassemble it within the province of Black Christians who lived in the urban North. (1993a, page 16)

On one extreme, black theology is another social movement, sometimes even godless, which seeks black liberation in the face of duplicity from the majority power structure. At the other end of the spectrum, black theology has been described as the attempt to worship God in a way that bypasses white intermediaries and is sensitive to the black experience in America. For some, theological or ecclesiastical failing is so oppressive along racial lines that any term which combines "black," "theology," and/or "Christianity" is welcomed – without respect to the content of the doctrine so labeled. The pain is so great that black theology adherents at each extreme refuse to criticize one another. Many put racial brotherhood above their own concept of theological correctness.

Afrocentrism is another movement which attempts to regain the self-esteem which was systematically taken from black people during the centuries of slavery and the century following. When one examines the artifacts of various cultures, one sees how they defined the world in terms of themselves. A prime example is how Mary, the Jewish mother of Jesus, is depicted as an Italian lady by Italian painters. When one considers that often our culture is our only frame of reference, one can understand why this may be done. At the same time, when such icons are used as an example of why God does not accept blacks, confusion ensues. The slaves had demonstrated that black people can discern when white people are being selective in teaching the Gospel. The Afrocentric movement demonstrates that sometimes the reaction is not the best. Afrocentrism attempts to replace a distorted Eurocentric view of Christianity with an equally distorted Afrocentric view. A friend shared a manuscript with me in which he describes the Pneumacentric church (Holy Spirit-centered church) as the only one revolving around the right center.

The Black Muslims are an interesting group. Afrocentric in worldview, they embrace an eclectic mix of Middle Eastern Islam, Christianity, Afrocentrism, and other influences. Characterized by inconsistencies from its inception, the Black Muslims were founded by a mysterious, little-known Wallace Fard, said to be a Turkish immigrant who preached, of all things, black supremacy. They were led by the Honorable Elijah Muhammad for many years. The Black Muslims grew to their peak in power under the tenacious assistant leadership of Malcolm X, who no doubt would have ascended to power had he not been assassinated years earlier. It needs to be noted, according to Carl Ellis (*Malcolm: The Man Behind the X*), that Malcolm seemed ready to turn the corner and head toward

Christianity just prior to his assassination. Upon Elijah Muhammad's demise, the mantle of leadership was passed to his son. As it stands, the younger Muhammad found that Mr. Louis Farrakhan had asserted his own claim to power and now exerts leadership over a large independent Black Muslim sect.

The Black Church is the most stable of the movements. It was conceived in an atmosphere of discrimination and dedicated to the proposition of responding to the one true God of the universe, the One who offers so great a salvation, so rich and free. Blacks never planned to develop separate Christian churches or denominations, but were forced to find their own form and place of worship during slavery and afterward. The St. Thomas Church, organized by Absalom Jones in 1794, was not allowed membership in the Pennsylvania Protestant Episcopal Diocese until 1865. Following slavery, black Christians were segregated in various meetinghouses and denied full participation. Finally, a number of black Christians decided that they might as well find their own place to worship. Thus began the American Methodist Episcopal (AME) denomination, which continues to this day.

The ensuing years have seen the formation of dozens of other denominations and smaller groupings, many of which have since folded. The black Church is an indigenized, contextualized expression of true Christian faith as understood and taught by their pastors and bishops, many of whom were/are self-taught or who learned by listening to other black and/or white preachers. The Black Church confesses allegiance to Christ. Black congregations tend to hold to a holistic expression of the Gospel, more or less, no doubt born out of their awareness of material as well as spiritual needs among their constituents. However, like so many white churches and denominations, a fair number of black churches and denominations have drifted from sound doctrine and moral living.

Modern day church growth proponents such as Peter Wagner have expounded the homogeneous unit principle, maintaining that churches grow faster when members have more things in common. The logical extension of Wagner's principle is that segregated churches grow best. While this may be true, Jesus' overriding principles include:

- love for other Christians and neighbors;
- conversion and discipleship;
- care for the less fortunate; and
- reconciliation.

To his credit, Peter Wagner has modified his position regarding homogeneous churches.

Conclusion

And what shall we say to those things? Africans did not sign up to come to the New World. Those who came as slaves suffered unparalleled atrocities and yet made an inestimable contribution to the settling of the Americas. Their descendants continued the legacy of pain under a number of political regimes. Too many good people did nothing to promote or to eliminate slavery and its successor, Jim Crow. Yet history bears almost mute testimony to the sacrifice of so many white, red, and black people to fight the sin that so easily beset this country in its infancy and even now in its third century of adolescence.

Through it all, the slaves learned to trust in Jesus. With the approval of the masters, the slaves learned the Gospel which reconciled so many of them to God through Jesus. In spite of the obstacles placed in their path, the slaves learned the parts of the Bible where God portrays Himself as the champion of the helpless. This kind of faith has been passed down through the generations so that many African Americans are the beneficiaries of that great legacy. It was the faith of our fathers and mothers that maintained some semblance of stability when all about them were losing their heads and blaming it on those of African descent. As modernity is running rampant in all sectors of the Church, it has come to the black community as well. Now we see various self-styled religious leaders trading on the black community's tendency to seek a god to "take their troubles to."

Yet even while Satan is having a field day in some sectors of the black community, he is not welcome in the Bible-believing churches. The banner of the Lord is still being raised in most black congregations all over this land. In most of the churches, people of good will of all races are welcome. There is ever an olive branch extended to those who seek to find the will of God for their lives.

References

Banks, William L. *The Black Church in the U.S.: Its Origin, Growth, Contribution, and Outlook.* Chicago: Moody, 1972.

Beals, Ivan A. *Our Racist Legacy: Will the Church Resolve the Conflict?* Cross Cultural Publications/Cross Roads Books, 1997.

Blackmon, Douglas. "Racial Reconciliation Beomes a Priority for the Religious Right," *Wall Street Journal*, Vol. 10, No. 121, CE/HL.

Bryant, T. Alton. "Ham," *The New Compact Bible Dictionary.* Grand Rapids:Zondervan, 1987.

Cone, James H., & Gayraud S. Wilmore (eds.). *Black Theology: A Documentary History*, Vol. I. Maryknoll, New York: Orbis, 1993a.

Cone, James H., & Gayraud S. Wilmore (eds.). *Black Theology: A Documentary History*, Vol. 2. Maryknoll, New York: Orbis, 1993b.

Ellis, Carl. *Malcolm: The Man Behind the X.* Intercultural Resources.

Epstein, I. (Ed.). *Hebrew-English Edition of the Babylonian Talmud* (Jacob Shacter, Tran.). (Rev. ed.). London:Soncino Press, 1969.

Felder, Cain Hope. *Stony the Road We Trod*: African American Biblical Interpretation. Minneapolis: Orbis, 1991.

Felder, Cain Hope. *Troubling Biblical Waters: Race, Class, and Family*. Maryknoll, New York: Orbis, 1989.

Figart, Thomas O. *A Biblical Perspective on the Race Problem*. Grand Rapids: Baker Book House, 1973.

Fitts, Leroy. *Lott Carey: First Black Missionary to Africa*. Valley Forge, PA: Judson Press, 1973.

Freeman, Joel A., and Don B. Griffin, with Eugene Seals (ed.). *Return to Glory: The Powerful Stirring of the Black Man*. Woodbury, NJ: Renaissance Productions, 1997).

Gaede, S.D. *When Tolerance Is no Virtue: Political Correctness, Multiculturalism and the Future of Truth and Justice*. Downers Grove, IL: InterVarsity Press, 1993.

Hesselgrave, David J. *Communicating Christ Cross-Culturally*. Grand Rapids: Zondervan, 1978.

"Ham," *International Standard Bible Encyclopedia*, Volume 2. Grand Rapids: Eerdmans, 1956.

Keil, C.F., & F. Delitzsch. "The Pentateuch," *Commentary on the Old Testament*, Vol. 1 (James Martin, Tran). Peabody, MA: Hendrickson, 1989.

Leo, John. "An anti-antiabortion rally," *U.S. News and World Report*. March 21, 1994.

Loewen, James W. *Lies My Teacher Told Me*. New York: Simon & Schuster, 1995.

McKissic, William D., Sr., & Anthony T. Evans. *Beyond Roots II: If Anybody Ask* (sic) *You Who I Am.* Wenonah, New Jersey: Renaissance Productions, 1994.

Perkins, John, & Thomas A. Tarrants, with David Wimbish. *He's My Brother: Former Racial Foes Offer Strategy for Reconciliation.* Grand Rapids: Chosen Books/Baker, 1994.

The New Lexicon Webster's Dictionary. New York: Lexicon Publications, 1989.

Pink, Arthur. *Gleanings in Genesis.* Chicago: Moody,1981.

Prinzing, Fred & Anita. *Mixed Messages: Responding to Interracial Marriage.* Chicago: Moody, 1991.

Robertson, A. T. *Word Pictures in the New Testament.*

Scofield, C.I. (ed.). *The Scofield Reference Bible: The Holy Bible.* New York: Oxford University Press, 1945.

Stitzinger, Michael F. *Notes on the Priesthood of the Believer & Soul Liberty.*

Thomas, Latta R. *Biblical Faith and the Black American.* Valley Forge, PA: Judson, 1976.

Vine's. *An Expository Dictionary of New Testament Words.*

Washington, Raleigh & Glen Kehrein. *Breaking Down Walls: A Model for Reconciliation in an Age of Racial Strife.* Chicago: Moody, 1993.

Webster's New World Dictionary. Collins, 1979.